Alan Harding

28. X.

THE RECORD SOCIETY OF
LANCASHIRE AND CHESHIRE

FOUNDED TO TRANSCRIBE AND PUBLISH
ORIGINAL DOCUMENTS RELATING TO THE TWO COUNTIES

VOLUME CXLII

The Society wishes to acknowledge with gratitude the support given towards
publication by

Lancashire County Council

ISBN 0 902593 73 0

Printed in Great Britain by 4word Ltd, Bristol

JACOBITES AND JACOBINS: TWO EIGHTEENTH-CENTURY PERSPECTIVES:

THE MEMOIR OF WALTER SHAIRP: THE STORY OF THE LIVERPOOL REGIMENT DURING THE JACOBITE REBELLION OF 1745

Edited by Jonathan Oates

AND

THE WRITINGS OF THE CRAGG FAMILY OF WYRESDALE

Edited by Katrina Navickas

PRINTED FOR THE SOCIETY
2006

FOR THE SUBSCRIPTION YEAR 2004

COUNCIL AND OFFICERS FOR THE YEAR 2004

President

J.R.H. Pepler, M.A., D.A.A., c/o Cheshire Record Office, Duke Street, Chester CH1 1RL

Hon. Council Secretary

Dorothy J. Clayton, M.A., Ph.D., A.L.A., F.R.Hist.S., c/o John Rylands University Library of Manchester, Oxford Road, Manchester M13 9PP

Hon. Membership Secretary

Maureen Barber, B.A., D.L.A., 7 Rosebank, Lostock, Bolton BL6 4PE

Hon. Treasurer and Publications Secretary

Fiona Pogson, B.A., Ph.D., c/o Department of History, Liverpool Hope University College, Hope Park, Liverpool L16 9JD

Hon. General Editor

Peter McNiven, M.A., Ph.D., F.R.Hist.S., The Vicarage, 1 Heol Mansant, Pontyates, Llanelli, Carmarthenshire SA15 5SB

Other Members of the Council

Diana E.S. Dunn, B.A., D.Ar.Studies   B.W. Quintrell, M.A., Ph.D., F.R.Hist.S.
B. Jackson, M.A., D.A.A.   D.A. Stoker, B.A., M.Ar.Ad.
V. McKernan, B.A., D.A.A.   T.J. Thornton, M.A., D.Phil.
C.B. Phillips, B.A., Ph.D.   G.J. White, B.A., Ph.D., F.R.Hist.S.
T.J. Wyke, B.A.

CONTENTS

GENERAL EDITOR'S PREFACE

The two parts of this volume are completely unconnected. They were offered separately, at about the same time, for consideration for publication by the Record Society. As originally presented, although both were of immediate appeal, they were each far too brief to stand as volumes on their own, and it was hoped that one or two texts of similar length might be found to join them in a Miscellany volume. However, Katrina Navickas was able to add a considerable amount of interesting material to her initial proposal. First, inspired partly by the Jacobite theme of Jonathan Oates's text, she added earlier memorandum book entries including references to the rising of 1715, as well as another Cragg family manuscript which was primarily conceived as a Quaker conversion tract but which touches on its writer's attitude towards Monmouth's rebellion of 1685. Secondly, the main text of the memorandum book, which Ms Navickas had originally edited to concentrate on matters of national political significance, was restored to its full extent, providing insights into more local economic and social conditions prevailing in the Wyresdale district of North Lancashire. Her introduction is very effectively complemented by her article 'The Cragg Family Memorandum Book: Society, Politics and Religion in North Lancashire During the 1790s', in *Northern History,* xlii (2005), pp. 151-62.

While the two contributions remain clearly distinct and do not even overlap in theme (in that they deal with different Jacobite risings), they illustrate between them some of the salient features of what might be called the 'long' eighteenth century; that is, the period from the 'Glorious Revolution' of 1688 to the French Revolutionary and Napoleonic Wars. The eighteenth century can seem a relatively featureless tract of British history, sandwiched as it is between the larger-than-life issues and personalities of the Tudor and Stuart eras and the dynamic and recognisably 'modern' Victorian period. In fact, its significance perhaps lies precisely in its status as a century of transition; a transition between a now quite alien world dominated by the personalities of monarchs and by dynastic politics and a modern period driven by more impersonal but at least as compelling political, social and economic ideologies. The enduring popular appeal of the 1745 Jacobite rising – a rising for which, as Jonathan Oates pertinently notes, the bulk of the history was written by the losers – surely represents romantic nostalgia for an era which had already passed when the rebellion took place.

It would in truth be difficult to find anyone less romantic or ideological than the Walter Shairp who presents himself to the reader of his *Memoir*. While he displays no sympathy for the Jacobite cause, there is not a trace of hostility towards 'the enemy', or indeed any hint of soldierly aggression, in his narrative. Even his desire to see the Jacobite prisoners in Carlisle seems totally lacking in malice or triumphalism: if any impression is given, it is one of almost friendly curiosity. On the other hand, Shairp gives no positive impression of patriotic or ideological support for the Hanoverian regime which Charles Edward Stuart aimed to over-throw. The nearest approach to a political stance comes in the innocuous state-ment that his regiment, the Liverpool Blues, was 'Rais'd to defend the Nation against the attempts made by the Son of the Chevalier de St. George in the Highlands...' Clearly Shairp was implicitly orthodox in upholding in his own per-son the Union of 1707 in the face of a threat to the status quo, and like many lowland Scots he presumably felt little or no affinity with his northerly compa-triots. It might be assumed that as a prominent member of the Liverpool business community his primary motive in volunteering for an active military role con-cerned the maintaining of stable trading conditions rather than the greater reli-gious, dynastic and international issues for which men were being asked to put their lives on the line.

Shairp was not simply an unthinking man in uniform slavishly following the commands of his betters. His account of his otherwise conscientious fulfilment of his duties is punctuated by occasional vigorous opinions on the shortcomings both of local civilians and superior officers. During the preliminary planning of the reg-iment's role, he rejoices 'at being no longer under the direction of a parcel of Ignorant aldermen', and describes a proposal of the ironically-designated 'Wise Corporation' as 'so Ridiculous a Scheme'. When the regiment was integrated into the overall strategy of the campaign against the Jacobites, Shairp and other offi-cers successfully challenged orders 'which ... appear'd so odd a Scheme ... that we could not help complaining of it'. As the prospect of direct contact with the enemy increased, Shairp and his fellow volunteers seem to have become less inclined to question the decisions of their commanders, although at the success-ful conclusion of their term of service he was at pains to record his frustration at the lack of recognition from the government which culminated in the disbanding of the 'best New Regiment raised in the kingdom ...& the very only one that had been of any service till then'.

Overall, however, Shairp's tone is one of contentment. 'I cant say that I ever before spent any time more agreeably ... ' 'For though we frequently had a great dale of Fatigue & trouble ... yet that was always made more than amends for the mirth & joy that we afterwards had when we got into our Quarters ...' The impres-sion is of a man at ease with himself who even managed to turn the extraordinary upheaval of the Jacobite rising into an affirmation of his values. Was he perhaps typical of a mid-century mood of slightly complacent satisfaction with the world which he inhabited?

The same could not be said of the main author of the Cragg memorandum book as he compiled his highly subjective record of the impact of international and national events on North Lancashire society. Much of Cragg's narrative deals with issues such as extreme weather, especially floods, with a distinctively sardonic coverage of crimes, scandals and other local newsworthy events. There is detailed material on the problems of the worsted mill at Dolphinholme and its impact on the region, illustrating the impact of the early stages of the Industrial Revolution and complementing the account by Benjamin Shaw published as volume cxxx (1991) by the Record Society. What really aroused Cragg's passions, however, was the juxtaposition of his sympathy with the French Revolution with his antipathy towards what he saw as the politically and fiscally repressive policies with which the British government was responding to the perceived threat to the established order.

Inspired by the increasingly forbidden writings of the radical Anglo-American political philosopher Thomas Paine, Cragg dismissed George III as a 'useless extravagant King or despot' and complained that 'we are now nothing but abject slaves subject to the will and caprice of a despotical tyrannical government' where 'Parliament is but a name, the Minister [William Pitt the Younger] rules them at his will and whatever method, whatever law he proposes, he carries it through ...' At the height of his hostility towards the government Cragg's views became explicitly treasonable as his wish for a revolution similar to that in progress across the Channel shaded into hopes that this might be effected through defeat for Britain in its counter-revolutionary Continental war. 'Let the French come and set up what sort of Government they please', he wrote, 'it cannot be worse than ours'.

The combination of righteous outrage and dark humour with which Cragg approached national politics was repeated at several more parochial levels. He described the local justices as 'overbearing and oppressive men [who] ...strain the Laws beyond their proper bounds'. He was dismayed at the economic suffering of the ordinary people as a result of the war's disruption of trade, and relished the discomfiture of greedy traders during food riots. He was contemptuous of the plethora of new taxes and enjoyed recounting the incidence of widespread and successful evasion in his own locality. Above all, he maintained an uncompromising hostility towards the local landowner whose role as 'tyrant of this neighbourhood' mirrored that of Pitt's oppressive central government. In Cragg's eyes John Fenton Cawthorne was incapable of anything but dishonourable intentions and actions. He supported the then highly controversial institution of slavery; he planned to enclose an extensive tract of common land in Wyresdale; he attempted to engineer the dismissal of the schoolmaster at Abbeystead; and he was embroiled in game disputes which in one case led to the shooting of three of his neighbour's dogs. It is almost unnecessary to record that the political affiliations of Cragg and Cawthorne were diametrically opposed. Cawthorne incited 'all the fools in the county', who 'very probably will go and pull somebody's house down for the good of the country and to shew their Loyalty to the King and Constitution' to demonstrate publicly against the opinions of Thomas Paine. In Cawthorne Cragg found a 'villain' who conveniently embodied what he saw as the unacceptable face of unreformed British society. The Quaker faith which underlay Cragg's political and social principles doubtless reinforced his suspicion of a hierarchical establishment and his opposition to the conscription of local men to fight in the militia.

Shairp and Cragg inhabited worlds which were only half a century apart but which were radically different. The relative stability of Shairp's era, only briefly disturbed by the aberration of the Jacobite rising, contrasts with the intense ferment of political, social and economic thought which spread from America (Cragg's 'land of liberty') and France to compel Britain to face 'the ambiguities and inconsistencies of a transitional period of history: where the older ideological world of the eighteenth century was being eroded by the new forces of a wider free market in both economy and politics, where class and nation existed but consciousness of them necessarily did not, but where the more ideologically certain world of the mid nineteenth century had not yet solidified to fill up the void.'[1] It may be unduly fanciful to see the phlegmatic Shairp and the 'angry' Cragg as typifying in their respective personalities the salient chararacteristics of these two contrasting periods. Whether or not this is the case, their accounts offer fresh perspectives upon what may still perhaps be regarded as an 'unfashionable' period of British history.

Peter McNiven

1 Katrina Navickas, 'The Cragg Family Memorandum Book', p. 152.

THE MEMOIR OF WALTER SHAIRP:
THE STORY OF THE LIVERPOOL
REGIMENT DURING THE JACOBITE
REBELLION OF 1745

Edited by Jonathan Oates

INTRODUCTION

The Jacobite Rebellion of 1745, the final armed attempt of the exiled Stuarts to regain the throne of Great Britain, is a very well known aspect of British history. Rarely a year passes without a new history appearing on the shelves. Yet though they vary in quality, most are similar in format; being yet another retelling of the old story of the military campaign from the Western Isles to Culloden, via Derby. The local angle to this key struggle is necessarily sidelined, as Charles Edward Stuart, his allies and his enemies take centre stage. This traditional approach, which began as the first books on the topic were published in 1746, seems unlikely ever to abate. However, this memoir concerns the activity of an anti-Jacobite volunteer force; the Young Pretender is only alluded to once, and, though the Duke of Cumberland is given a little more of the canvas, his role herein is essentially peripheral. The introduction to this memoir, never previously published, which was written by a junior officer in the volunteers, has a number of aims. It will briefly summarise the Jacobite rebellions, with special attention to the North West in 1745, before proceeding to introduce the memoir and the memoirist himself. Then the role of the regiment will be surveyed and the value of the memoir discussed.

The Jacobite Rebellions, 1689–1746

The Catholic James II went into exile in December 1688 after being ousted from his throne because of the combination of a successful invasion by William of Orange and the fact that he had managed to antagonise much of the Protestant political nation, even though only a minority acted against him. From 1688 to the 1750s, he, his son and his grandson all tried to regain the throne he had lost. Although the Stuarts often had foreign backers, usually France, Britain's main commercial and imperial rival, there were those in Britain who were sympathetic to their cause, especially in Scotland, but also some (the exact number is unknown and the extent variable and disputed) English Tories and Catholics who were supportive. These people were known as Jacobites, after the Latin for James, Jacobus.

Published history concentrates very strongly on the 1745 rebellion, and, since this is the rebellion which this memoir concerns, the following paragraphs will concentrate upon it. But it does not seem remiss to sketch in the main points of the earlier part of the Jacobite struggles. The first attempts were made in Scotland and Ireland, but despite initial success at Killiecrankie in 1689, the Jacobites were defeated. James II died in 1701 and his son, James Francis, took his mantle. There was an invasion attempt in 1708, but this was foiled by the Royal Navy. A more serious effort occurred after the accession of the first Hanoverian monarch, George I. Given the lack of instrinsic loyalty to the new German monarch, and resentment in Scotland due to the recent imposition of the Act of Union (1707), this appeared very dangerous to the new dynasty and its Whig supporters.

Certainly, large numbers of men were raised for the rebellion, especially in Scotland, but also in England. A mixture of bad luck, poor intelligence, faulty communications and military incompetence on the part of the Jacobites helped to doom the cause, and led to the battle encounters being disappointing from their point of view. James did arrive in Scotland, but it was probably too late and he failed to make much of a positive contribution.

The next thirty years were largely unsuccessful for the Jacobites. There were a number of conspiracies – the Gyllenborg Plot of 1717 and the Atterbury Plot of 1722 – as well as an invasion attempt on the part of the Spanish in 1719, but none of these ever came close to being the threat posed by the Fifteen. However, James had married and his first son, Charles Edward Stuart, was eager to have his father crowned King. His chance appeared to have come in 1744. With Britain and France mortal antagonists in the War of Austrian Succession (1740–48), Louis XV of France thought that a cheap way of knocking out his rival would be to assist Charles in invading England and imposing his father upon the throne. An army was assembled in 1744 and Charles arrived at the quayside, only to learn that the Royal Navy and storms in the Channel made an invasion impossible.

The young man was not deterred. In July of the following year, with only seven companions, he took two ships to Scotland. One was turned back by the Royal Navy, but the other, in which he was travelling, arrived off the coast of Scotland. The Forty-Five had begun. Support in Scotland was mixed. Yet a couple of thousand clansmen joined him; enough to worry the government, who slowly recalled troops from the Continent and ordered Sir John Cope to take his small force into the field against him. Liverpool was aware in mid-August that a rebellion had begun, and, Whiggish town that it was, formulated a loyal address to the King, assuring him of its loyalty, in the following month. Volunteer troops were raised thereafter.

Charles's force took Edinburgh without a struggle and then went on to rout Cope's army at Prestonpans on 21 September. This had many important consequences. For the Jacobites, it meant control of Scotland, save for a few outposts. Recruits swelled their ranks and an invasion of England was being discussed. But, just as importantly, their opponents began to redouble their efforts in opposition towards the rebellion. As well as recalling more military units, loyalty to George II began to make itself manifest in the counties and cities of England. There were loyal addresses, money was raised and volunteer units were formed. Regular troops marched to Newcastle upon Tyne and to the Midlands, since it was not known by which route the Jacobites would march into England, if indeed they were going to attempt an invasion at all.

On 8 November, the Jacobite army crossed the border and began to besiege Carlisle. However, Scottish Jacobites were only half-hearted in the invasion – the vote to invade had been by a margin of one. Yet, at least at first, everything went well. Carlisle fell, volunteer and militia forces faded away and Marshal Wade's army at Newcastle failed to intercept them. Even though the Jacobites were marching through Kendal, Lancaster, Preston and Wigan, it was still uncertain where their ultimate destination would be. They might march to Wales to pick up support there and join up with any French forces which might land there, or they might march to London via Derby.

The Liverpool forces were ordered to try to hold up the Jacobites until the regular forces in the Midlands could march against them. This meant that they should block or destroy bridges and the like. The bridges across the Mersey were therefore crucial. If the Jacobites wished to march to Wales, the direct route would be via Warrington. Or, if they wished to keep their foes uncertain as to their movements, they could march to Manchester and take the route to Wales via Altrincham. If their plan was to march to London, the bridges south of Manchester were the important ones. The Warrington bridge was partially demolished, but the Jacobites marched south-east from Wigan to Manchester and then south-east again, towards Derby.

At Manchester, about two hundred recruits swelled Jacobite ranks. As the march continued southwards, they evaded Cumberland's forces and reached Derby on 4 December. London was only 123 miles away; perhaps little over a week's march. Cumberland's and Wade's armies were not within striking distance. Charles was eager to advance. Yet his council were not – principally because they had received very little support from either England or France. There was also concern that the combined numbers of their foes far outnumbered them. Despite Charles's entreaties, his council decided that a retreat was the only sensible option. En route, they left a garrison at Carlisle, which was taken by the pursuing troops (including the Liverpool Blues, who had briefly sheltered in Chester) under Cumberland.

The Jacobites managed to retreat to Scotland, and enjoyed a number of successes, at Falkirk on 17 January 1746 and over a number of loyalist Scots forces and garrisons. Cumberland's army, well trained and well supplied, marched northwards and confronted a badly fed, demoralised – yet unbeaten – Jacobite army on Culloden Moor on 16 April 1746. The Jacobites were defeated and their rout was complete. After the battle, Charles gave up the immediate struggle and the rising was effectively over. Though there were further plots and invasion schemes in the 1750s, none came to anything. James died in 1766 and his son in 1788. Jacobitism was over – but it had been a long and lingering demise. [1]

Shairp's Memoir

Much of our first-hand knowledge of the Forty-Five comes from accounts written by those intimately involved in it. Published memoirs of various protagonists of the Forty-Five rebellion are certainly not uncommon. There are seven well-known narratives produced by Jacobite officers which have been published and have been widely used by historians. [2] They help to give, intentionally or other-

1   B. P. Lenman, *The Jacobite Risings in Britain, 1689–1746* (London, Eyre Methuen, 1980).
2   R.F. Bell, ed., *The Memorials of John Murray of Broughton, 1740–1747* (Edinburgh, T. & A. Constable for the Scottish History Society, 1898); W.B. Blaikie, *The Origins of the Forty Five* (Edinburgh, T. & A. Constable for the Scottish History Society, 1916); B. Rawson, ed., *The Chevalier de Johnstone: a Memoir of the Forty Five* (London, Folio Society, 1958); E. Charteris, ed., *Lord Elcho: an Account of the Affairs in Scotland in the Years, 1744–1746* (Edinburgh, James Thin, 1907); R. Forbes, ed., *Jacobite Memoirs* (Edinburgh, Chambers, 1834); A. and H. Tayler, eds., *The 1745 and After* (London, Nelson, 1938); J. Maxwell, *Narrative of Charles, Prince of Wales' Expedition to Scotland in the Year 1745* (Edinburgh, pr. T. Constable, 1841).

wise, a Jacobite interpretation of events, and many historians have happily followed in this vein. As Speck has noted, in the case of the Jacobite rebellions, contrary to popular myth, it is the losers who have, by and large, written the history books, not the winners. [3] Published accounts by those opposed to the rebellion are less common and have been under-used. They are all by civilians; such as the diary of Richard Kay, Lancashire doctor, and that of William Jessup, a Holmfirth apothecary (both Dissenters) but generally speaking, it is the Jacobites whose accounts of the rebellion are best known. [4]

The correspondence of those loyal to King George survives in voluminous amounts at the National Archives (primarily in State Papers Domestic), at the British Library (primarily the Newcastle and Hardwicke Mss) and at County Record Offices (such as Leeds Archives). These are top-down versions of events. Most of these were from Lords Lieutenants and other relatively senior figures, and since they are largely unpublished, are relatively inaccessible, and indeed, unknown to most save for academic historians.

It needs to be stated that opposition in England to the rebellion was widespread, though it has often been overlooked or dismissed by historians because such forces as were raised did not, because they could not and were not expected to, confront a vastly larger Jacobite army in battle. Throughout England, a great number of loyalist associations were formed and many of these, especially in the northern counties of England, formed bodies of volunteer troops, usually infantrymen. What is known about these forces comes mainly from the correspondence of the Lieutenancy and from the local and national press. This is either history from above or the official reports in the press. Such sources are inevitably partial, though important.

Later conflicts such as the French Revolutionary and Napoleonic Wars produced a number of memoirs from junior officers and from men from the ranks, though chiefly from those in the regular army, which was employed abroad. [5] Yet none seem to have been written by volunteers during the Forty-Five, except for men serving with the British Army, and these latter are accounts of the rebellion itself, as much as personal memoirs. In any case, they are heavily reliant on contemporary newspapers for much of their content. [6]

Except one, that is. The Memoir of Walter Shairp was unknown to Rupert Jarvis, who wrote a large number of articles about the North West of England during the

---

3   W.A. Speck, *The Butcher: the Duke of Cumberland and the Suppression of the Forty Five* (Oxford, Blackwell, 1995), p. 1.

4   C.E. Whiting, ed., *Two Yorkshire Diaries,* Yorkshire Archaeological Society, 117 (1952); W. Brockbank and F. Kenworthy, eds., *The Diary of Richard Kay, 1716–51, of Baldingstone, near Bury, a Lancashire Doctor,* Chetham Society, Third Series, 16 (1968).

5   J. Selby, ed., *The Recollections of Sergeant Morris* (London, Longmans, 1967); C. Hibbert, ed., *A Soldier of the Seventy First* [Thomas Pococke] (London, Leo Cooper, 1976); C. Hibbert, ed., *The Recollections of Rifleman Harris*, new edition (London, Leo Cooper, 1970).

6   M. Hughes, *A Plain Narrative and Authentic Journal of the Late Rebellion* (pr. for Henry Whitridge, 1746); J. Ray, *A Compleat History of the Rebellion* (York, printed for the author by John Jackson, 1749).

Forty-Five, including one article surveying Liverpool during the rebellion. [7] Nor was Frank McLynn aware of it, writing much later. [8] The only published authors to use it were Don Higham in the following decade, [9] and, to a far lesser extent, the present editor in his more recent unpublished doctoral thesis and in an article about the second siege of Carlisle. [10]

It was whilst working on this thesis that my attention was (quite by chance) brought to the Memoir, which is housed at Liverpool's Merseyside Maritime Museum, and is accessible to all (there is also a photocopy at Liverpool City Library, Acc. 2379). It appears, however, to have been severely under-used, perhaps because it has only recently been housed at the Museum. [11]

The provenance of the journal is not wholly clear. It eventually reached the hands of one John Wilson, book seller of Eynsham, Oxfordshire. He sold it to the Merseyside Maritime Museum in, perhaps, the 1980s. How it came into his possession and what happened to it after being written, is a mystery which we are unlikely ever to solve. In a sense, of course, it does not matter. What matters is its survival.

Walter Shairp

The memoirist himself was not an important figure during the rebellion, as were many of the Jacobite memoirists, such as Lord George Murray, Jacobite lieutenant general, and John Murray of Broughton, Charles's secretary. [12] This means that he was not privy to the meetings of the great and good, nor even to the councils of war which his colonel held, as they would only have been attended by the senior officers, captains upward. Yet this gives his memoir the value of being, relatively, one describing events from the 'bottom up'.

Walter Shairp was a lieutenant in Captain Spencer's company of Liverpool Blues, raised by the city during the emergency. This is noted in the latter pages of the memoir. Yet, at first he appears to be a difficult man to track down. His memoir seems to reveal no personal details as to his home, family, profession or age. It solely concerns the period of the rebellion, and is in no way an autobiography. However, a little research, using the methods well known to the experienced geneaologist, has uncovered a number of facts about him and his antecedents.

---

7 R.C. Jarvis, *Collected Papers on the Jacobite Risings, I* (1971).

8 F.J. McLynn, *The Jacobite Army in England, 1745: the Final Campaign* (Edinburgh, Donald, 1983).

9 D. Higham, *Liverpool and the '45 Rebellion* (Birkenhead, Countryvise, 1995).

10 J.D. Oates, *Responses in North East England to the Jacobite Rebellions of 1715 and 1745*, Reading University PhD, 2001; Oates, 'The Last Siege on English Soil: Carlisle, December 1745', *Transactions of the Cumberland and Westmorland Antiquarian and Archaeological Society*, New Series, III (2003), pp. 169–84.

11 Liverpool Merseyside Maritime Museum, DX 594 (Liverpool Central Library Acc. 2379).

12 Bell, *Murray of Broughton*; Forbes, *Memoirs*.

The Shairp family, foremost of whom was William d'Escharpe, came over to Scotland from Normandy during the reign of David II of Scotland, in the early fourteen century. In the sixteenth century, John Shairp was advocate for Mary, Queen of Scots, and built a family residence, Houston, at Uphall, West Lothian. One of his descendants, another John, was advocate to James VI and was knighted for services rendered. Moving forward to the eighteenth century, there was Thomas Shairp, an M.P. for Linlithgowshire, 1700–07 in the last Scottish Parliament and fiercely opposed to the Union of 1707. The family produced merchants, soldiers, lawyers and bankers. [13]

Thomas had no sons. His daughter, Janet, married her cousin, also called Thomas Shairp (c. 1698-c.1771), son of Captain Walter Shairp of Blanes (b.c. 1660). They had at least two sons; Thomas (1721–81), the eldest (who inherited the estates) and Walter. Therefore, far from being from Liverpool, or Lancashire, or even England, Walter was baptised at the presbytery in Uphall on 9 December 1724. He attended Edinburgh University, matriculating in 1740. By early 1744 at the latest he was transacting business in Liverpool on his father's behalf. This included scouring Lancashire to procure hounds for Lord Hopetoun, discussing the sugar trade of Jamaica, being concerned over rising insurance costs of shipping due to the war with France, and considering the possibility of investing £500 in a privateering enterprise now that Britain and France were officially at war. He seems to have been well acquainted with other Liverpool merchants, such as Mr Heywood, who is specifically mentioned in the only surviving letter from Shairp from this period. He was probably in Liverpool at the time of the rising and therefore associated with fellow merchants who formed his brother officers in the Liverpool Blues. [14]

Shairp remained in Liverpool for some time after the end of the rebellion, becoming a member of the Liverpool Ugly Face Club. He became a merchant based at St Petersburg in 1748. On 7 April 1752, at the British chaplaincy in that city, he married Eleanora Lindeman. They had about nine children; Jennet (born 1755), Margaret (1753–54), Eleanor, Catherine, Thomas Charles (born 1756), Stephen (born 1757), Walter (died 1811), Alexander (who was baptised in Scotland) and Alice. From 1777 he was His Majesty's consul general to the British Factory, being knighted at some point for his services. His daughter, Alice was married in 1783; Catherine and Eleanor also married. In 1797, Stephen took over his father's position in Russia's capital city, returning to Britain in 1805 where he was knighted. Alexander also remained in Russia until 1813. Walter's business took him outside Russia for much of 1757–66; letters being written from London, Hull, Hamburg

---

13 National Archives of Scotland, GD1/1311/13, 21; 30/2049/1, 11; *Burke's Landed Gentry*, II (1848), p. 1222.

14 NAS, GD30/1583/1–2; International Genealogical Index; M.D. Young, ed., *The Parliaments of Scotland*, II (Edinburgh, Scottish Academic Press, 1993), pp. 631–2; information from Edinburgh University Library.

and Amsterdam. Walter Shairp died on 8 August 1787, though he does not seem to have left a will. A successful life and career, though not a spectacular one. [15]

Unfortunately, there is no known portrait of Shairp in existence. The only information we have about his appearance comes from a jaundiced source. As noted above, he was a member of 'The Most Honourable and Facetious Society of Ugly Faces', which existed in Liverpool from 1743 to 1754. Shairp's physical qualifications were noted thus 'A disproportionate forehead', 'Eyebrows little or None', 'Rough unpolished face', 'Thick large bottle Nose', 'Odd cast with his eyes', 'Large Mouth, and an excellent grin'. Several of his fellow officers in the Liverpool Blues, as shall be noted, also belonged to this Club. [16]

There is much that we do not know, and will probably never know for certain, about Shairp. Did he experience any initial hostility during the period of the rebellion because of his being Scottish? There was rampant, though understandable, 'Scotophobia' in the press and from the pulpits in England during the period of the rebellion. [17] Yet he was probably an accepted member of the Liverpool commercial community by 1745, being within the charmed circle of merchants, though a relatively junior one, due to his age. Why was he so strongly anti-Jacobite that he felt the need to take up arms against them? He could have merely given money to pay for others to do so. No reason is given. Though his maternal grandfather was anti-Union in the 1700s, his brother Thomas refers to being threatened by Lord George Murray with military execution if money was not paid to the Jacobites. He was probably a Presbyterian (he was presumably baptised at the Uphall presbytery, the only church in that place), so he would have been antipathetic to the rebellion on religious grounds. Furthermore, merchants were often opposed to the disruption to commerce which the rebellion threatened, and some were not averse to taking action. Additionally he may have had a young man's fancy for a soldier's life. As Dr Johnson noted 'Every man thinks meanly of himself for not having been a soldier'. [18]

It may seem curious that Shairp, as a Scot, was so opposed to the rebellion that he took up arms against it. His fellow memoirist, James Johnstone, was also a Lowland Scot, from a merchant family, though his inclination was to serve with the Jacobites. [19] Yet Shairp was by no means unique in his behaviour. Many Scots opposed the rebellion of 1745, and many fought against it, either in the independent companies raised in the Highlands, or, rather more effectively, in regiments of the British Army at Culloden. [20] Nor was Shairp the only Scot to join a predominantly English volunteer unit. George Clerk left Scotland in the wake

---

15 NAS, GD1/1311/13; GD30/1583/8–26; IGI; *The Gentleman's Magazine* (1783), p. 804; (1787), p. 838; (1795), p. 1060.
16 E. Howell, *The Ugly Face Club of Leverpoole, 1743–1754* (Liverpool, 1912), p. 37.
17 Speck, *Butcher*, pp. 186–7.
18 NAS, GD1/1854/12; J. Boswell, *The Life of Samuel Johnson* (London, David Campbell, 1992), p. 815.
19 Rawson, *Memoir*, p. 17.
20 Speck, *Butcher*, pp. 183–5.

of the Jacobites taking Edinburgh and joined the Yorkshire Royal Hunters, a unit of volunteer cavalrymen formed at York in September 1745. [21] Yet, crucially, Shairp was the only one to have written an account of his experiences.

The Liverpool Blues

In response to the danger posed by the Jacobite Rebellion of 1745, several corporations, as well as counties, in the north of England formed volunteer units. York, Berwick, Newcastle and Hull were four of these, Liverpool was a fifth. At first, the arrival of Charles in Scotland in July 1745 was not credited as a serious danger. However, even before the Jacobites had routed Sir John Cope's troops at Prestonpans on 21 September, the potential danger was apparent to many in the north of England as well as the government. England had enjoyed decades of peace and distrusted standing armies. However, with armed rebellion in Scotland, which could soon turn into an invasion of England, the civilian authorities had to turn to military force to protect themselves and to show their loyalty to the status quo in State and Church.

These volunteer units were not the militia. The militia could not legally be raised because the counties had not been reimbursed the money owing to them. Therefore George II, acting through his principal Secretary of State, the Duke of Newcastle, granted mayors the power to form bodies of uniformed and armed volunteers in quasi-military units, and gave them blank commissions, in order to appoint officers. [22] Militarily inexperienced gentry and merchants usually filled the ranks of the officers; disbanded soldiers made up the NCOs, whilst townsmen and countrymen of lowly birth made up the rank and file, usually glad of the fixed income (higher than that of private soldiers in the regulars, with less danger and a limited period of service). [23]

Money to pay the men and to purchase uniforms and other necessities came from public subscriptions. There would be an official meeting, and sums of money would be promised by people of all ranks. They would then be asked to pay in instalments. Arms were often a problem, and had to be procured from the Tower of London; often a lengthy and bureaucratic procedure. [24]

It has already been stated that their task was not to take on the Jacobite army, which vastly outnumbered these relatively small units. In part their duties were ceremonial – taking part in loyalist celebrations. They were in part political – to demonstrate loyalty to the government. They were also there in a police role – to suppress any local outbreaks of Jacobitism, to arrest suspects and to carry out searches for arms. They were also called upon to assist the regulars. [25]

---

21 W.A.J. Prevost, 'Mr George Clark and the Royal Hunters', *Transactions of the Cumberland and Westmorland Antiquarian and Archaeological Society,* 63 (1963), pp. 231–52..
22 Oates, *Responses*, p. 47.
23 Ibid., pp. 227–8.
24 Ibid., pp. 47–52, 223–5.
25 Ibid., pp. 238–44.

Although many different regiments of volunteers were raised during the Forty-Five, the Liverpool Blues stands out, since other units raised by corporations did not venture beyond their city walls. This did not happen in Liverpool. While the County Militia did not serve outside the county boundaries, the Liverpool Blues served in Cheshire, Westmorland and Cumberland as well as in Lancashire. James Ray of Whitehaven, a contemporary historian and volunteer in Cumberland's army, writes with some justification, as well as pride, that 'there was no Regiment in the campaign, that made a better appearance than the Liverpool Blues'. [26]

The Liverpool Blues, as the regiment was called, has received some comment from historians, after Ray's flag-waving account of it in his *Compleat History of the Rebellion*. Rupert Jarvis was the first twentieth-century writer to give it some attention, using Liverpool Town Books, State Papers and the regimental records of the Liverpool Blues, which he found among the Theyer papers. Unfortunately the whereabouts, and even the survival, of the latter is, at present, unknown; anyone making these documents (or even copies) public, would be doing a great service. Jarvis discussed the constitutional issues surrounding the regiment, its raising and equipping, and its role in destroying bridges in the county. He has only the sketchiest comments to make about its service in December 1745. [27] Even McLynn, often dismissive of English irregular opposition to the Jacobites, states 'The voluntary force formed on Merseyside, the 'Liverpool Blues', though it never saw action, was one of the success stories of the Whig side in the '45'. [28] As we shall see, it did see action, but McLynn's point is valid nonetheless. The best and fullest account comes from Higham, who has examined the issue from a number of sources. [29]

The Memoir as History

Shairp's Memoir is a unique document in more than the sense that every archival document is unique. It is the only surviving history written by a member of the myriad English volunteer forces raised in 1745 to combat the rebellion. It is not certain when it was written; probably some time in the decade after the events described, but to be more certain than that is not easy. The handwriting of the Memoir is more akin to that in the letters of 1744 and 1748 than the handwriting of letters written in the 1750s and onwards. However, in the notebook which contains the Memoir, the year 1754 is noted.

We do not know why he wrote it. Shairp may have decided to make a record of such exciting events, either for his own sake, as part of taking stock of his life shortly after his arrival in Russia, or, if he wrote it in 1754, just after his marriage,

---

26 Ray, *Compleat History*, p. 130.
27 Jarvis, *Collected Papers I*, pp. 246–7.
28 McLynn, *Jacobite Army*, p. 6.
29 Higham, *Liverpool*.

it may have been for the sake of his wife and family. It certainly was not for a wider audience – since it was not published, as many soldiers' memoirs were after the Napoleonic Wars. Presumably it was for private readership only. Shairp does not make much reference to himself – the first person is scarcely used. Nowhere does he draw attention to his own exploits, except in a very ordinary fashion. He is very far from being an egotist. Nor does he pretend to be a chronicler of wider events. Unlike the accounts of Hughes and Ray, mentioned earlier, he does not try to write about the whole campaign, largely leaving the press to do so. We do not know what he felt about the wider campaign, nor about any distaste which he may have felt about acting in opposition to fellow Scots (assuming that he did feel any kin to rebellious Highlanders – as a Lowlander living in England he may have shared the English outlook). Although there were many Lowlanders in the Jacobite army, Shairp always refers to 'the Highlanders'. Rather, Shairp writes merely of what he experienced and what he had seen at first hand. If there is a hero, it is the Liverpool Blues themselves. Shairp's sense of pride and achievement comes from being a part of that regiment.

The Memoir gives the reader a wholly new perspective on the campaign of the Forty-Five. The first few pages describe the formation of the regiment and their initial experiences whilst in Liverpool. At the beginning of November, two regular officers arrive to take command. Much to the distaste of Liverpool's corporation, the regiment leaves the town. Whilst at Warrington, they receive their first order – to destroy the bridge there, which would impede the Jacobites' marching towards Chester and Wales. This having been accomplished, the troops are then told to destroy the bridge at Crossford. Again, this is dealt with.

However, with the arrival of the Jacobites at Manchester, the regiment moves to reinforce the garrison at Chester, their stay at which is not a happy one. With the Jacobites' retreat from Derby, the regiment is back in action again, and spends mid-December in marching northwards through Lancashire, Westmorland and Cumberland. It is here that they see action at last. The Jacobite garrison at Carlisle is holding out, and the Duke of Cumberland finds the regiment to be useful in blockading the town. The town and castle fall without any need for a potentially bloody assault, as happily noted by Shairp. The regiment then marches back to Liverpool and is disbanded, though without the government's recognition which Shairp thought it merited.

The account adds to what we can already learn from other manuscript sources, newspapers and contemporary histories. Nowhere else is there an account of what it was like to be a soldier in a volunteer unit on active service during the rebellion. We learn of the hardships endemic even in the life of a volunteer soldier; of early rises, miserable billets and hard marches, of the inclemencies of a winter campaign, the risks of making an assault and the lack of praise from an ungrateful government (though Shairp never doubts that Cumberland had a high regard for their little corps).

Yet all is not gloom. Shairp, like many soldier memoirists, looked back with fond memories of his time in the ranks. It is especially interesting to note this, because as a Scot he may have been the subject of suspicion and prejudice – some

Englishmen deemed all that was Scottish to be evil, but clearly this was not so in this instance. Why else would he talk of the 'mirth and joy' which they shared after marches, or why would he find himself invited into gentlemen's houses? He also took a great pride in his unit, again not uncommon among soldiers throughout the ages. Rifleman Harris, who endured many hardships during the Peninsular War, later noted 'I can only say that I enjoyed life more whilst on active service than I have ever done since...the only part worthy of remembrance'. [30]

Shairp was not a historian, nor a published author. Yet his writing has many merits. He seems to be lacking in prejudice against his country's enemies. Writing several years after the end of the rebellion, he can afford to be detached, but he has also remembered the events he recounts. He does not speculate or discuss events which he did not witness. He gives facts and feelings only. Nor does he shy away from the miseries of a military life. Yet he does not complain or whinge unreasonably. Nor are there any bombastic statements, high-flown rhetoric or moralising. His account is a model of concision. As soon as the unit is disbanded, little more is said. It is a regimental history, not another history of the rebellion (of which several had been published by the 1750s). As far as can be ascertained from other sources, Shairp's Memoir is factually accurate. Of course, for much of what he writes, there is no other source.

Shairp is not perfect, of course. His account does err on the side of discretion when it comes to his beloved regiment – there is a reference in the Cumberland Papers that James Higginson and Thomas Norris of the Liverpool Blues were found to have stolen a pair of shoes and stockings each, and it is also on record that four men of the regiment stole ammunition from Lieutenant Gildert at Chester. [31] He refers to Major Bendish as William, though other sources call him Richard. [32] He also states that his colonel received an express on 20 November to say that the Jacobites had arrived at Kendal, yet they did not do so for another two days, and then only the advance guard. But this could be due to faulty intelligence, not Shairp's memory.

The memoir is written in a small notebook, 15 cm in height, 11.5cm in width and about 1cm thick. The script is in a firm hand, and copious loops appear therein. Shairp's memoir contains many abbreviations. It is possible that his manuscript was a first draft, since there are occasional crossings out. His spelling is also erratic by modern standards. There are footnotes to people and events mentioned in the text, in order to make matters clear to the reader. All dates are given in Old Style. The original spelling and punctuation has been retained throughout. Apart from the text of the memoir, there are some miscellaneous notes within Shairp's note book. I have included the cures for animals, but have omitted a number of routes (one being 'A Root from Houston' to Liverpool), listing towns and the distances between each.

30 Hibbert, *Harris*, p. 106.
31 Royal Archives, Cumberland Papers, 8/69; Cheshire Record Office (CRO), DCH/X/9a, Order Book.
32 Anon, *The Army List of 1740*, Society for Army Historical Research, no. 3 (Sheffield, W.C. Leng, 1931), p. 35.

Further Reading

Readers eager for campaign histories of the Forty-Five are spoilt for choice, but the following are particularly recommended; W.A. Speck, *The Butcher: The Duke of Cumberland and the Suppression of the Forty Five* (Oxford, Blackwell, 1981); F.J. McLynn, *The Jacobite Army in England, 1745: The Final Campaign* (Edinburgh, Donald, 1983); S. Reid, *1745: a Military History of the Last Jacobite Rebellion* (Aberdeen, Spellmount, 1996); and C. Duffy, *The Forty Five*, (London, Cassell, 2003). Those interested in aspects of the rebellion as regards northern England should note the works already referred to by Jarvis and Oates, and J. D. Oates, *The Jacobite Invasion of 1745 in North West England* (Lancaster, Centre for North-West Regional Studies, 2006).

Acknowledgements

I wish to express my thanks to Don Higham, Dr Alan Crosby and Dr Stephen Taylor for their help and advice in this undertaking. I also wish to thank the staff of the Merseyside Maritime Museum Library (Shairp's Memoir is reproduced courtesy of National Museums Liverpool, Merseyside Maritime Museum), the Royal Archives, West Lothian Archive Service, the National Archives of Scotland and Liverpool Central Library for their assistance with my queries. But most of all, I thank Walter Shairp for having had the sense of mind to record, however briefly compared to Jacobite memoirists, his own experiences. History sometimes can be written by the victors, even modest and humane men such as Shairp, and it is to his agreeable company that I leave the reader.

JONATHAN OATES, 2006

THE MEMOIR OF WALTER SHAIRP

Liverpool Merseyside Maritime Museum
DX 594
Liverpool Central Library Acc. 2379

(1r) A History of the Raising & adventures of the Liverpool Regiment of Blues. This Regiment was caled from the Colour of their Cloaths which was Blue turn'd up with Red. [1] It was Rais'd to defend the Nation against the attempts made by the Son [2] of the Chevalier de St. George [3] in the Highlands of Scotland [4] by the Corporation [5] & Inhabitants of Liverpool upon Subscription [6] which were begun to be taken in about the first of Octr 1745 [7] and the Commissions [8] were granted (2v) to the officers [9] who were to Command it the 4th of Octr & against the 10th & 11th. There were officers & men for six companys [10] amongst which I was

1 Blue uniforms were also worn by the Yorkshire Association volunteers, the Yorkshire Royal Hunters; Swiss troops employed against the Jacobites also wore blue, as did the French Royal Scots who fought with the Jacobites. (S. Reid, *1745: A Military History of the last Jacobite Rebellion* (Aberdeen, Spellmount, 1996), p. 44).

2 Charles Edward Stuart (1720–88), the Young Pretender or Bonnie Prince Charlie, titular Prince of Wales, after 1766 Charles III. He arrived in Scotland in July 1745. (*ODNB*, 11, pp. 145–55).

3 James Francis (1688–1766), the Old Pretender, or the titular James III and VIII. (Ibid., 29, pp. 613–18).

4 Charles arrived on Eriskay, one of the Western Isles, on 23 July. (F.J. McLynn, *Bonnie Prince Charlie* (Oxford U.P., 1991), p. 128).

5 A Charter of 1695 enabled Liverpool to be governed by a corporation of mayor, aldermen and common councillors. The total number was reduced to 40 (W. Farrer & J. Brownbill, eds, *The Victoria History of the County of Lancaster*, IV (London, Constable, 1911), p. 27).

6 Subscription schemes to raise money to pay for volunteers or for recruiting to the regular army occurred throughout the country. Subscribers promised to pay a total sum, and then paid it in instalments as requested. (J. Oates, *Responses in North East England to the Jacobite Rebellions of 1715 and 1745*, Reading University PhD, 2001, pp. 223–5).

7 A meeting held on 20 September resolved that men should be raised; the King gave his permission for this three days later and the order to put this into action occurred on 29 September. According to Ray, £6,000 was raised by subscription (£2,000 out of public stock, the remainder by the city merchants). However, Picton opines that £4,589 was raised, though he later states it was 'upward of £6000'. Certainly, £3,000 was raised on 29 September. According to Ray, there was great enthusiasm for such a project 'the chearfulness and Alarcity with which every one contributed to the forwarding of this noble Design; Since even the poorer sort did not refuse to cast in their Mite, and the rich were not slack in giving according to their Abilities'. (J.Ray, *The Compleat History of the Rebellion* (York, printed for the author by John Jackson, 1749), p. 126; Sir James A. Picton, *Liverpool: Municipal Archives and Records from A.D. 1700 to the Passing of the Municipal Reform Act 1835* (Liverpool, Walmsley, 1886), p. 110; The National Archives, State Papers 36/68, ff. 179r, 281r, 69, ff. 233r-234v).

8 Thomas Holles, the Duke of Newcastle (1693–1768), Secretary of State, wrote, on 23 September, giving the Mayor permission, through the King's Sign Manual, 'to grant commissions to such persons, as he [the Mayor] shall think proper'. This was common practice in other towns and counties where such volunteers were raised. Only the King could grant such powers to corporations and counties. (W.S. Lewis, ed., *Yale Edition of Horace Walpole's Correspondence* (London/Oxford, Oxford U.P., 1937–83), 30, p. 445; TNA, SP36/68, f. 281r; *ODNB*, 27, pp. 722–30).

9 A list of the officers can be found in the Appendix, p. 33. According to Ray 'they had not been bred in the military way, being mostly gentlemen, tradesmen, &c.' (Ray, p. 130).

10 There were later seven, and finally eight companies, as will be noted. The actual number of men is disputed. According to Graham there were 'about 500 as good men as could be tempted'. Picton claims that they numbered 648; Ray puts the figure at nearly 700; *The General Advertiser* gives 'nearly 800'. The Corporation had hoped to raise 800 or 1,000. (Ray, p. 125; Picton, *Municipal Records*, p. 108; TNA, SP36/69, f. 234v, 73, f. 263r; *The General Advertiser*, 5350, 19 Nov. 1745).

made a Lieutenant. Ever after that time we were imployed in Disciplining [11] the Soldiers by their diffr't Companys in which they made very great progress & now & then lining the streets in Honour of the Mayor [12] & Corporation upon any Publick Days [13] which was all that was done worth Notice. (2r) Excepting our continually Inlisting & Discharging our men at the Pleasure of the Corporation who were excessively unsteady in their resolutions until the 10th Nov when Colonl. Graham [14] & Coll. Gordon [15] two pritty Gentlemen & very good Soldiers came down to command the Regiment by his Majesty's orders and to our great happiness & joy at being no longer under the direction of a parcell of Ignorant aldermen. (3v) Upon Monday the 11 Novr the Coll order'd all the 6 Companys to parade by day light in the Town field [16] which we did & had our arms [17] deliver'd outt & he drafted out of all the Companys to reduce them to 70 Private Men which drafted he formed into a Compy for his Nephew Mr Ben. Heywood [18] the 12th. Nothing Extraordinary hapened only the Mens hatts, shoes & stockings (3r) were deliver'd to them. The 13th he reviewed them and putt them through the Manuall Exercise & firing with which he was greatly pleased & gave a very good character of the Officers. The 14th nothing was done with the Regiment but a

---

11 Military exercise, such as marching and drill. Discharged sergeants and corporals put the men through their paces. (TNA, SP36/69, f. 235v).
12 Owen Pritchard, merchant, (d.c.1765) was Mayor in 1744–45; John Brooks his deputy. (TNA, SP36/68, f. 179r, 69, f. 233r; W.F. Irvine, ed., *Wills at Chester, 1761–1780*, II, R.S.L.C., 38 (1899), p. 24).
13 Probably these were the anniversary of George II's Coronation (11 October), his birthday (30 October) and 5 November (the anniversary of the 1605 Gunpowder Plot and the arrival of William in 1688). (Oates, pp. 333–4).
14 Lieutenant Colonel William Graham (d.1747), of Kirke's battalion of Foot. Colonel of the Liverpool Blues. promoted to Brigadier, 1746. (Anon, *The Army List of 1740*, Society for Army Historical Research, no, 3 (Sheffield, W.C. Leng, 1931), p. 16; C. Dalton, *George I's Army* (London, Eyre & Spottiswoode, 1910), p. 137).
15 Lieutenant Colonel Alexander Gordon of Fielding's battalion of Foot, Lieutenant Colonel of the Liverpool Blues. However, Thomas Brerton, a Liverpool M.P., claimed that Gordon was of the Marines. (*Army List*, p. 46; TNA, SP36/69, f. 234r).
16 Townfield was that expanse of fields and cultivated land that lay to the east of urban Liverpool from the Middle Ages to the early nineteenth century. (R. Stewart-Brown, 'The Townfield of Liverpool, 1207–1807', H.S.L.C., 68 (1916), p. 24).
17 These weapons were muskets, probably with bayonets, and probably from the Tower of London. Newcastle informed the Board of Ordnance on 18 October that 800 arms were to be sent to Liverpool; on 26 October, he added that ammunition, sixteen drums and twenty-four halberds were also to be sent there. Graham noted giving these weapons to the men on 11 November. In August 1745, the corporation of Liverpool only had 220 muskets, 154 pistols and 25 swords in its stores. On 29 September, Pritchard noted the need for the loan of such weaponry. (TNA, SP44/132, p. 423; SP36/73, f. 263r; Picton, *Municipal Records*, p. 105; TNA, SP36/69, f. 235v).
18 Captain Benjamin Heywood (1712–95) (7th Company of the Liverpool Blues). a merchant of Liverpool. He and his brother Arthur later founded Liverpool's first bank. Shairp had had business transactions with him in 1744. Also a member of the Ugly Face Club. (H.A. Ormerod, 'Extracts From the Private Ledger of Arthur Heywood', *Lancashire and Cheshire Historical Series*, 103 (1951), p. 103; Picton, *Memorials of Liverpool*, II (London, Longmans, 1875) p. 152; National Archives of Scotland, GD30/1583/1; E. Howell, *The Ugly Face Club of Leverpoole, 1743–1754* (Liverpool, 1912), p. 65).

Resolution was made by the Wise Corporation yt we should lye in town to defend it against the Enemy [19] which was so Ridiculous a Scheme thatt itt had like (4v) to have putt an end to the whole as Coll Graham was so much displeas'd att the town offering to force him into such a command & refusing to lett him have the sole management of the men thatt he had like to have left them all together & all the officers were determin'd to lay down their commiss if they had nott leave to march wherever the Coll thought propper as it was with (4r) that view that they had all enter'd into the scheme & nott to defend the town in particular. However, upon second thoughts they gave that up & left the whole to the Collonel who march'd us out of town the 15th when the men were all cloath'd & arm'd. We got no further than Prescott [20] that night as it was late before we got out of town & most of the Men were got Drunk by (5v) the Generosity of their friends at parting. From Prescott we went in the morning to Warrington the 16th were we gott the soldiers very well Quarter'd & lay there the 17.18 & 19th without any thing Extraordinary hapning. The 20th about two in the morning the Coll receiv'd advice by Express of the Enemy having gott to Kendall [21] & about six the Drum bet to arms to get us all to the Parade in the Corn (5r) Markett From whence we march'd about eight of clock with an intent to go & join Sir Jn. Ligonier [22] the main Body consisting of 6 Compys wentt to Northwich about eight miles that day & Capt Campbell's [23] Compy with all the Baggage went to Stone that night and nixt day to Newcastle [under Lyme]. The 20th the 6 Compys lay at N. Wich & the Collonell went with Capt Heywood (6v) to Northwich expecting to meet some of the Generall Officers or to learn whereabouts the army lay but could get no Inteligence of them however. He receiv'd orders from Sir Wm Young [24] to return to

19 According to Ray, there was discussion within the corporation as to whether the troops should be used to guard the city (as the volunteers raised in the cities of York and Newcastle did) or be used to reinforce the regular army. According to him 'However, on mature Deliberation, when they reflected, that to provide for their own private security, when that of the Publick was at Stake, was mean and ungenerous, they unanimously agreed to send them to reinforce the Royal Army'. In any case, the corporation instituted a system of patrols to safeguard the city at night. (Ray, p.126; Picton, *Municipal Records*, p. 108).

20 Marching eight miles a day might be creditable for tipsy men, but the Jacobites could march twice that. (B. Rawson, ed., *The Chevalier de Johnstone: A Memoir of the Forty Five*, (London, Folio Society, 1958), p. 60).

21 According to John Murray of Broughton, the Jacobites' advance guard reached Kendal on 22 November, followed the next day by their main body. (R.F. Bell, *Memorials of John Murray of Broughton*, 1740–1747 (Edinburgh, T. & A. Constable for the Scottish History Society, 1898), p. 245).

22 Lieutenant General Sir John Ligonier (1680–1770). Of Huguenot ancestry, he was appointed to command that part of the British Army sent towards the Midlands, but was superseded on 26 November by the Duke of Cumberland. (*ODNB*, 33, pp. 769-72).

23 Captain George Campbell (d. c. 1769) (5th Company of the Liverpool Blues), sugar merchant and shipowner, Mayor of Liverpool 1763–64. He was involved in transporting Jacobite prisoners to America after Culloden. (Picton, *Memorials*, II, p. 293; Irvine, *Wills at Chester, 1761–1780*, I, R.S.L.C., 37 (1898), p. 52).

24 Sir William Yonge, Secretary at War (c. 1693–1755), responsible for direction of battalions, finance and supply. On 19 November, he wrote to Graham to tell him to defend the bridge at Warrington and generally to obstruct the Jacobites' march. (*ODNB*, 60, pp. 82–3; TNA, WO5/37, p. 168).

Warrington. This Night Lieutt. Farmer [25] came up & join'd us with Capt. Colquitts [26] Compy wch was raised after we left Liverpool. Nixt morning being the 22d the 7 companys marched of for Warrington (6r) about 9 of clock & got there att Noon where we found that our orders were to pull down the Bridge & defend that pass as well as we were able this Night Capt Campbells Coy came up to us upon pres'd horses butt left the Baggage at Newcastle which was very unlucky as none of us had any Cloaths with us but what were upon our Backs so Mr Todd [27] was sent nixt morning to bring it up. (7v) The 23d we lay at Warrington all day & about noon Brigar Douglas [28] came to Consult with the Coll and Mr Blackburn of Orford [29] who din'd there & after dinner the Brigar Return'd to Chester this night our Major Willm Bendish [30] came to us. About 2 o Clock nixt morning 24th the Coll receiv'd an Express [31] from Chester & att 5 begun to pull the Bridge down at 8 we march'd the Batalion over the Bridge & with 10 men out of each comany to assist (7r) at puling it down & about eight att night we had two of the middle arches quit down [32] this night our men were very ill quarter'd

25 Of Captain Colquitt's Company; possibly J. Farmer of the Ugly Face Club (Howell, p. 65).
26 Captain John Colquitt (d.c. 1773) (8th Company of the Liverpool Blues); Collector of Customs at Liverpool from 1725. As Collector, he was responsible for safekeeping the 'public money', i.e. the customs fees which he collected. Given that the sums in his hands in late 1745 were considerable (in early November, he had almost £2,700 in his keeping), and because it was customary for the rebels to confiscate these on entering towns they passed through, he had an anxious time in November 1745. He moved his family to Cheshire at this time. His money and documents, along with those of the corporation and other merchants, were probably put aboard one of the Royal Navy vessels then lying off Liverpool. He was still in Liverpool on 19 November, but after then only returned on 14 and 31 December. (Picton, *Memorials*, II, p. 279; R.C. Jarvis, *Collected Papers on the Jacobite Risings*, I (New York, Barnes and Noble/Manchester U.P., 1971), pp. 219–20; Jarvis, *Customs Letter Books of the Port of Liverpool, 1711–1813*, Chetham Society, Third Series, 6 (1954), pp. 63–4; Irvine, *Wills at Chester, 1761–1780*, R.S.L.C. (1898), p. 64).
27 Ensign in Captain Heywood's company. (See Appendix 1, p. 33).
28 Sir William Douglas (d. 1747); once Colonel of the 30th Foot. Ordered to command the troops at Chester, under Cholmondeley's supervision, in November 1745. (C. Dalton, *George I's Army*, p. 179; TNA, SP36/73, f. 327r).
29 This could be a reference to one of three men. John Blackbourne of Orford the elder (1691–1787) was a botanist (J. Aikin, *A Description of the Country from Thirty to Forty Miles Round Manchester* (London, printed for John Stockdale, 1795), p. 307). His son of the same name (1721–68) attended Queen's College, Oxford, and was Sheriff of Lancashire in 1763. (J. Foster, *Alumni Oxonienses, 1715–1886*, I (London, Joseph Forster, 1887), p. 117). The other was Ireland-Blackburne (Farrer & Brownbill, eds, *VCH Lancashire*, III (1907) p. 147).
30 Presumably Shairp is in error about Bendish's Christian name. Major Richard Bendish of Peer's Foot is presumably indicated. Bendish is also referred to as Richard by Picton. (*Army List*, p. 35; Picton, *Municipal Records*, p. 109).
31 On the 25th the Earl of Cholmondeley, Lord Lieutenant of Cheshire (see n. 47), told Newcastle that 'I sent to Warrington last night, for the breaking down of that Bridge'. There was some local opposition to such demolition work, on the grounds that it would be ineffectual. (British Library Additional Manuscripts, 32705, f. 375r; Royal Archives, Cumberland Papers, 7/142).
32 Colquitt was responsible for the demolition of the bridge. Two shillings was spent in bringing ladders from Warrington and for sinking boats, presumably to deny the Jacobites any

as we were oblig'd to canton them in the little village on the Cheshire side of the River. I had the good fortune to get very good quarters at one Mr Halls [33] a little country sqr who had two very pritty Daugrs. Nixt morning I was sent as Quarter Master to Frodsham. I met with the Colonel & Brigr Douglass coming (8v) Chester for Latchford where they order'd Capt. Tongue's [34] & Capt Heywood's Compays to lye & Guard the Bridge & had a Breastwork rais'd upon the end of it. The other 6 Compays came into Frodsham about 4 o Clock where I mounted Guard all night during all this time we had expresses coming with news from the rebells who were now advanced as far as Preston. [35] Nixt day being the 26th about 7 o Clock the Drum beat (8r) to arms & between 9 & 10 we marchd outt under command of Brigr Douglas & Capt Colquitt Compys went for Latchford to Relieve the other two under command of Coll Gordon the 5 remaining compys march'd that night to Stockport wch was 21 computed miles they all got in very late & as I commanded the rear Guard it was 1 o Clock before they all came up as we were very much retarded by pressing & bringing up the Tools to pull down the Bridges although we press'd cartes & horses for the men from Altringham (9v) which is Six miles from Stockport. Our old vigilant Coll had the Drums beting by 5 nixt morning & threatn'd to putt all the Officers under arrest for not appearing upon the parade as soon as himself without making any Indulgence for the fatigue we had had the Day before but we got the men out at last after great trouble & sent 10 out of each company to pull down ye Bridge which was don that day about 10 o Clock [36] the Brigr gave orders for 2 Compays to be (9r) Detach'd to Crossford Bridge a place about 6 miles off wch Lott fell upon our Compay & Capt Masons [37] who both went off immediately & got to the place appointed about 1 o Clock at Noone when we begun to that piece of work which our men were now growen

possibility of using local materials to cross the river at this point. (Jarvis, *Collected Papers*, I, p. 246).

33 His identity is unknown. He does not appear in the Chester Poll Book of 1747, nor in the lists of University alumni. Possibly he is Thomas Hall, Esq. of the Hermitage (d.c. 1747). (J.P. Earwaker, ed., *Wills at Chester, 1741–1760*, R.S.L.C., 25 (1892), p. 78).

34 Captain William Tongue (1st Company of the Liverpool Blues). (See Appendix 1, p. 33).

35 According to the Chevalier de Johnstone, the van of the Jacobites arrived at Preston on 25 November and their main force on the following day. Murray claimed they were 'mett by a great Course of people and welcomed with the loudest shouts and Acclamations'. However, John Daniel states that 'notwithstanding all our proposals and exhortations, few of them consented to join the Prince's Army'. (Rawson, p. 54; Bell, pp. 245–6; W.B. Blaikie, *Origins of the Forty Five* (Edinburgh, T. & A. Constable for the Scottish History Society, 1916), p. 169).

36 Ten masons, four carpenters and two labourers were employed on this task. The labourers were paid two shillings, the skilled men three shillings and sixpence. Nineteen shillings and four pence was spent on drinks for the men; eight shillings on food and another 4s 4d on more drink. Finally, 1s 9d was used to hire a horse to take a lame man home. (Jarvis, *Collected Papers*, I, p. 84).

37 Captain Peter Mason (3rd Company of the Liverpool Blues), landwaiter in the Customs in Liverpool. (D. Higham, *Liverpool and the Forty Five* (Birkenhead, Countryvise, 1995), p. 114).

very alert att & fond of as it was mischief however the Bridge was so well built that & our Tooles so blunted that it stood us till six the nixt morning altho' it had but one arch when we receiv'd an order from the Brigr (10v) and Coll Graham who lay that night att Altringham to leave of working which was don accordingly butt it was so far cut down that the whole Bridge fell in half an hour after we left it. All the last night & this day the 2 coms under command of Coll Gordon were imploy'd in pulling down Barton & another wooden Bridge & were now return'd to Latchford. This Morning the 28th Coll Graham set out (10r) to wait upon the Duke of Cumberland [38] at Litchfield & the Brigr return'd to Chester Our 2 Companys after geting a little refreshment at Altringham were join'd by the other 3 from Stockport. We were here informed that the advance party of the Highlanders had come into Manchester last Night [39] & that their Drums were heard this morning which was but 5 miles of us. So we march'd all the 5 Compys out about 12 o Clock 2 of them (11v) Vizt Stewarts [40] & Campbells went under comand of Maj Bendish to Lime that night intending nixt morning to relieve the 3 at Latchford with Coll Gordons the other 3 Coys, viz Spencer [41] Mason & Weakleys [42] went to High Lee to be att Frodsham the Head Quarters nixt day when we Came there the men were pritty well Quarterd all about in the Country houses & the officers were Receiv'd very civilly by Mr Lee [43] a Gent of Fortune (11r) in thatt place & were all invited to sup & lye that night at his house which gave us all great joy. I had at that time got little or no sleep for the 3 nights by past. But alace what a disagreeable message did we Receive just as we were

38 William Augustus (1721–65), Duke of Cumberland, second son of George II and Commander in Chief of the British Army. Defeated the Jacobites at Culloden on 16 April 1746. (*ODNB*, 59, pp. 105–13).
39 The Jacobites arrived at Manchester on 29 November. Daniel comments about 'The ringing of the Bells, and the great rejoicings and salutations with which we were welcomed, gave us mighty expectations'. Murray adds 'a good many of the Towns men enlisted'. Certainly about 200 men, their only substantial source of recruits from England, did so, though far more were hoped for. They formed the 'Manchester Regiment' led by a Catholic Lancashire gentleman, Francis Townley (1709–46), who had seen service in the French army. Yet local non-Jacobites were alarmed; as Kay wrote 'O, How Persons are removing their Families and Effects out of Manchester'. (Blaikie, p. 171; Bell, p. 246; W. Brockbank and F. Kenworthy, eds, *The Diary of Richard Kay, 1716–51: of Baldingstone, near Bury, a Lancashire Doctor*, Chetham Society, Third Series, 16 (1968), p. 102).
40 Captain Francis Stewart (4th Company of the Liverpool Blues), Tide Surveyor in Customs at Liverpool. Colquitt notes he was given leave of absence from his post, from 10 November to 22 January, due to 'there being little prospect of any business going forward at that time' (Jarvis, *Letter Books*, p. 66).
41 Captain Lawrence Spencer (2nd Company of the Liverpool Blues), merchant and shipowner; Deputy Customer in Customs at Liverpool; Mayor of Liverpool, 1759–60. During an invasion scare in 1759, he formed a number of volunteer companies, uniformed in blue. Member of the Ugly Face Club. (Picton, *Memorials*, I, p. 190, II, p. 64; *Gore's Liverpool Directory* (Liverpool, Gore, 1766), p. 7; Howell, p. 65).
42 Captain Isaac Wakeley (d.c. 1758) (6th Company of the Liverpool Blues), office holder in the Customs at Liverpool. (Earwaker, *Wills at Chester, 1741–1760*, p. 192).
43 Probably Sir Peter Leigh, Esq., of Lyme. His father, who died in 1744, had been a staunch Jacobite. (Chester Record Office, Chester Poll Books and Election Pamphlets, 1747–1827, I, p. 21; C. Duffy, *The Forty Five* (London, Cassell, 2003), p. 65).

sitting down to a very elegant supper we Receiv'd a letter from Maj Bendish inclosing Co Gordons orders for us all to come directly to Warrington Bridge to defend that Pass as he had been informed that a party of (12v) the Highlanders were to be in town that Night so we gave orders for the Drum to bett to arms & after eating a little with the good Gentn, we march'd all the men off with great Spirits they all expecting to have a Battle that night & about 12 o clock we got to Latchford where we found all the other 5 compys. That night instead of Mr Lees comfortable logings that we made ourselves so happy in expecting we were forced to put up with a Dale floor & some (12r) times a chair to sleep in the men provid'd themselves the best way they could in Barns & Stables. Nixt morning we found the information we had got was false as no Highlanders appear'd on ye the other side however we heard by a man who came over from the town in the only Boat that was then within some miles of us & had been amongst them at Preston & Wiggan that they certainly intended to come to Warrington & he believed the main body would be there. (13v) Against 12 o Clock this day upon that Information we caled a Councill [44] having first made a strict inquiry into the mans Character & found it to be very good from severall of the most creditable people in the place we concluded that itt was not safe for us to lye any longer there as the frost & had so lowered the River that it was fordable in severall places both above & below (13r) us and as so small a Body as ours lying there could be of no service in opposing the whole army when there was no Forces near us to support us in case we were bet from the Post. About half an hour after we were informed from the other side that considerable party of the Enemy had been within 2 miles of us but were since turned of towards Manchester. We got that afternoon about 4 o Clock to Frodsom where (14v) we greatly alarm'd by a Drum beting the March out of town which was first heard by our Serjeant Major [45] as he was going to fix a Guard upon ye Bridge who as soon as he heard it came in a great hurry to the House where the officers were quarter'd & inform'd us that he had heard the march over the hill and Believed the Highlanders to be at hand upon which we all got ourselves ready as (14r) soon as was possible sett the Drums a beting to arms & in 15 minus we march'd 400 men down to the Bridge wch was most that we had in town the rest being all quarter'd in the country & there we found it to be a false alarm rais'd by a Boy who was learning to bet & had gon there for that purpose However this was of som service to us as it gave us an opportunity of trying the mens courage which was very extraordinary as not a (15v) man of them show'd the least sign of fear but went all on with the greatest alarcity altho' I believe every one of them expected to be attacked that moment the Lieut Coll & Major were very well pleas'd with their behaviour. We fixed a Guard that night of 100 men att the Bridge house. Nixt morning we Receiv'd orders from Brigr Douglas for one of the Companys to Return to Latchford to

---

44 A council was a meeting of the officers to decide on the best course of action – a standard
    military procedure.
45 There is no clue to his identity.

defend the Bridge & (15r) other 2 Compys to march to North Wick which when we heard appear'd so odd a Scheme to the whole Core of officers that we could not help complaining of it & layd the blame of it all upon Lord Cholmondely [46] as we wer told that he was very much avers to our Coming into his Garrison of Chester for fear of the high pay [47] our men had raising som disturbance in his new Regiment & we had Reason to believe he had ben very (16v) instrumental in hindering us from joining the Kings army & likeways that he had talked very freely of our Regiment in generall for which Reasons we had contracted a great dislike to him as we looked as upon our Regiment to be greatly superior to his. We therefor Resolv'd to show som little spirit and not allow ourselves to be made Fooles of or throwen into danger where we could not be of any Service (16r) *[the name is crossed out]* drew up a Remonstrance to Brigadr Douglas wch Coll Gordon took to Chester complaining of its being very hard for us to be tossed all over the Country & not suffer'd to join any other force when the enemy was so very near us & more that they would not even allow us to keep together but scater'd us all about the Country in small parties which render'd us quit Defensless against (17v) the most inconsiderable atack we Concluded with telling him that we thought if our service was not thought worth accepting we did not think it worth ofering only desir'd he would let us know that we might lay down our arms in the same manner as we had taken them up as we did not choose to throw ourselves away foolishly & be of no use at the same time by doing it (17r) This Night we Receiv'd a letter from Coll Graham at N. Wich ordering us to march the whole Batalion to that place & ther to waite the Dukes further Comands & same we had a litter from C. Gordon with an acct of the Success of our Remonstrance which had had the intended effect as he got leave from Ld Cholmondley to march us into Chester [48] however at that time we dispised that liberty as the order we had got from the Duke was much more agreeable (18v) But in the Night time we had a second order from Coll Graham Countermanding ye first as he thought it dangerous to lye at North Wich having had Certain intelligence of the Highlanders crossing the Mersey by a wooden Bridge they had thrown over near Crossford so in the morng about 10 of Clock we march'd for Chester having been first joined by Capt Masons Co which had gon to defend the (18r) Pass at Warrington & about 3 we got into Chester along wth the 2 Comps thatt were order'd to N. Wick viz Campbells and Weakly's. When we came in there which was on the 1st of Decr we found the

46 George Cholmondeley (1703–70), 3rd Earl of Cholmondeley, governor of Chester Castle and Lord Lieutenant of Cheshire. (*ODNB*, 11, pp. 506–7).
47 The privates in the Liverpool regiments received twelve pence per day and four pence extra for each day spent away from home. Most volunteers received twelve pence without any additional allowance. (Liverpool Town Books, Liverpool Central Library, 2/5, p. 379). On 15 November, Newcastle had suggested that the Blues help in the defence of Chester, but Cholmondeley thought that this was 'very improper'. (CRO, DCH/X/9a/5, 7).
48 Yonge's orders to Graham on 19 November were for him to 'retire to Chester' if the Jacobites marched southwards en masse. (TNA, WO5/37, p. 168).

City & Castle was putt in the best posture of Defence that was possible [49] as itt was believed by every Body that ye Highlanders design was to march through that place in their Road to Wales [50] where they expected a great many would (19v) joyn them. [51] The Troops that lay there were Bligh's Regiment of Foot [52] Ld Chomleys [53] & Ld Goores [54] 2 New Regiments with whom we did our turns of Duty by keeping Constant Strong Guards in the City with them which was all yt we did extraordinary while we lay there excepting one day that the Regiment was marching upon the Roads by Ld Chomley who was very well pleas'd with our performance. During that time the Highlanders (19r) had march'd as far as Derby. [55] At Stone they had very nigh gott past the Dukes Army [56] but by his care and vigilance in marching by night to Swansons Bridge Pass that they were necessitated to be masters of before they could go any further he turned them there and from that time forward they never offer'd to look south ward again.[57] (20v) The 11th Decr we Receiv'd orders from the Duke to march to Latchford to defend the Old Pass at Warrington Bridge & we gott 2 small cannon for that purpose to preventt the Enemy from returning [58] that way while ye Duke followed them with his Horse so about 12 o Clock that day we march'd out of Chester as also did Brigar Blighs Regiment to joyn the army & got to Frodsham (20r) about 5 o Clock

---

49 Chester was an important walled city with a castle, and its garrison was reinforced with two battalions from Ireland during the rebellion. Even so, there were doubts about its state of defence. The Blues began guard duty there on 1 December. (TNA, WO5/37, p. 55; W.A. Speck, *The Butcher: the Duke of Cumberland and the Suppression of the '45* (Oxford, Blackwell, 1995), p. 85; CRO, DCH/X/9a/8–9).
50 Reviewing the situation of 4 December, Cumberland certainly thought he had once wondered whether the Jacobites had planned to march into Wales. (Royal Archives, Cumberland Papers, 7/287).
51 Sir Watkin Williams Wynn, M.P. (c. 1693–1749) was the principal Jacobite in Wales, and had been involved in plotting a restoration prior to the rebellion. Some historians think he may have set off to join the Jacobites with a retinue in early December, but there is no concrete evidence of this. (F.J. McLynn, *The Jacobite Army in England, 1745: The Final Campaign* (Edinburgh, Donald, 1983), p. 131).
52 The 20th Foot, present at Carlisle and Culloden. (Blaikie, *Itinerary of Prince Charles Edward Stuart* (Edinburgh, T. & A. Constable for the Scottish History Society, 1897), p. 98). For Brigadier Edward Bligh (1685–1775) see *ODNB*, 6, pp. 213–14.
53 One of the newly raised regiments formed during the rebellion. See n. 91.
54 Lord Gower's regiment.
55 The Jacobites reached Derby on 4 December. (Bell, p. 248).
56 The Jacobites outflanked Cumberland's army, which was at Lichfield, by a ruse. Their advance guard moved to Congleton, resulting in Cumberland, believing this to be the harbinger of the Jacobites' main force, moving his army to Stone, allowing the main force to arrive at Derby. (Bell, p. 247).
57 On 5 December, the Jacobite leaders discussed an advance on London. The main reason for not doing so was stated as the lack of support in England and from France. The issue has been endlessly debated by historians, but, as with all hypothetical scenarios, it can never be satisfactorily resolved, For a good summing up of the arguments, see Duffy, *The Forty Five*, pp. 300–13. The retreat began on 6 December. (R. Forbes, ed., *Jacobite Memoirs* (Edinburgh, Chambers, 1834), pp. 54–5; Rawson, p. 65).
58 The Jacobites returned via Macclesfield and Manchester, retracing their route southwards. (Rawson, p. 65).

where we halted till 11 when the Coll gave orders for marching that Night to Latchford & so sett out in a very Dark Cold Night & gott in about 3 in the Morning. I went to my old Quarters at Mr Halls which was extreamly good for the place we were at as the men were almost all starv'd with Hunger & Cold having no quarters but what they could gett in Barns and Stables. Nixt morning the (21v) the Regiment was drawn up & 3 Compys were order'd to stay at the Bridge & the other 5 were sent into the Country to be canton'd in the Neighbouring Villages & to be ready at a call while we lay there the Duke Cross'd the River about four miles above us with all his Cavalry [59] in pursuit of the Enemy who it was certain were now making the best of their way back again for Scotland. So as there was (21r) no further occasion for our lying at Warrington Bridge the Coll sent Mr Mc Gough [60] off to the Duke for further orders who came back on Saturday night with orders for the Coll to march us to Preston & lye there till he had occasion for us. Nixt day being the 15th we cross'd ye River by a flatt & about 11 o Clock march'd out of Warrington for Wiggan where we gott in at 3 & about 5 o Clock came in 1000 Volunteers outt of the Guards & other marching Regiments [61] (22v) & Brigr Bligh's Regiment which with our men were all the infantry of the Ds Army. The Cause of their Returning that night as they had only march'd out in the morning & gott half way to Preston was a report the Duke had heard of 15 Thous French being landed in the south which may be reasonably said was what prevented our army from overtaking the Highlanders as it threw them a days march behind. [62] We all lay that night (22r) in Wiggan & were very much pinched for want of Room. In the morning we march'd for Preston along with the other Troops & got all in there safe about 3 in the afternoon where we found the first of the Rebels that was executed hanging in the Markett place whom the Duke had seen tyed up that morning before he left the town as he had Deserted from Sir J. Cope's army after the Battle of Prestonpans & joyned them [63] We halted all the next day in Preston as also did the rest of the foot that came in wth us and spent the day

---

59 On learning that the Jacobites were in retreat, on 8 December Cumberland set out with his mounted troops to pursue. These regiments were as follows: Bland's Dragoons (3rd Horse), Ligonier's Horse (7th Dragoon Guards), Kerr's Dragoons (11th Horse), Cobham's Dragoons (10th Hussars) and Kingston's Horse (disbanded). The total has been estimated at 1500. (Blaikie, *Itinerary*, p. 94).
60 John McGough, member of the Ugly Face Club. (Howell, p. 40), or Colonel Graham's batman (information supplied to editor by Don Higham).
61 Cumberland's command included ten battalions of Foot and three battalions of Guards (perhaps 7,000 men in all). (Blaikie, *Itinerary*, p. 94).
62 A French invasion force, variously computed as 12–15,000 in number, was in readiness at Dunkirk. Although enthusiasm among the French high command for the invasion was lukewarm and divided, Newcastle and Lord Hardwicke, the Lord Chancellor, who were in London took it very seriously and the former wrote to Cumberland on 12 December to order Ligonier to return to London with his battalions. Cumberland himself halted his forces at Macclesfield. According to Ligonier 'I find the apprehensions of a foreign invasion save the rebels'. (RA, CP, 8/9, 20).
63 Lieutenant General Sir John Cope (c. 1700–60), Commander in Chief in Scotland until his defeat at Prestonpans on 21 September 1745. Several men who deserted from Guise's regiment after Prestonpans and joined the Jacobites were hanged in 1746. The most famous

in receiving the mens arms and ammuniton making more Cartridges for them. Nixt morning we all receiv'd orders to march for Lancaster & got there about 4 at Night when Brigar Bligh[64] who comanded the foot receiv'd orders from the Duke to press horses [65] & march them all but our Regiment to Kendall with the outmost expedition which (23r) was accordingly don in the dark but they were there too late to be of any service as it was about the time we got into Lancaster that the Scirmage was fought at Clifford [66] which is upwards of 30 miles off. This Night & the two following Days we lay in Lancaster & did nothing extraordinary but mounted a Capts Guard at the end of the Bridge & an subs in town till on Saturday the 21st of Decr we Receiv'd an order from the Duke. (24v) About noon to march for Penrith directly & there wait his further orders. This order came at a very unreasonable time as we had had all the men under arms a little before but were then dismissed wch made it very difficult to get them all out again however the Coll hurried away with a part of them the rest followed after they all reached Burton that Night. Nixt day we march'd very early for Shap & gott in there late after a most (24r) fatiguing march which was occasion'd by our haulting in Kendall as we went through & the badness of the Roads as they are the worst that are in this part of England. We were very badly quarter'd that night & set out nixt day to Penrith where we got ourselves pritty well refresh'd but got orders to march in ye morning to Stanwick Banks a small village on the other side of Carlisle at the end of (25v) the Bridge there to defend the Pass & prevent any of the Enemy from making their escape that way as we had information of 500 [67] of them being left there while the Duke was to besiege the town wch he had now invested. [68] And accordingly we sett out from Penrith in the morning where I left my horse

deserter turned Jacobite was Allan Breck Stuart, hero of Robert Louis Stephenson's *Kidnapped* and *Catriona*. Cumberland had a deserter turned Jacobite hanged at Macclesfield, too. (*ODNB*, 13, pp. 314–15; A. Livingstone, C.W.H. Aikman, B.H. Hart, eds, *Muster Roll of Prince Charles Stuart's Army* (Aberdeen U.P., 1984), p. 215; McLynn, *The Final Campaign*, p. 154).

64 See note 52 above.
65 The army had no transport of its own, and had to use that of civilians. For a discussion of army transport, see Jarvis, *Collected Papers*, I, pp. 48–74.
66 This was the skirmish at Clifton Moor, near Penrith on 18 December. Lord George Murray, Lieutenant General of the Jacobite army, held off Cumberland's advance guard, the latter retaining the field of battle. (Rawson, pp. 69–70; R.S. (Chancellor) Ferguson, 'The Retreat of the Highlanders through Westmorland in 1745', *Transactions of the Cumberland and Westmorland Antiquarian and Archaeological Society*, X, 1889, pp. 186–228).
67 The Jacobite force actually numbered about 400; two escaped, one or two may have been killed during the siege, 396 surrendered, viz., 114 Englishmen from the 'Manchester Regiment', 274 Scots from a number of non-clan regiments and eight Frenchmen. Their leaders were John Hamilton and the forementioned Townley. Their remaining at Carlisle was a highly controversial decision and is hotly disputed in the memoirs of rebel officers. (TNA, SP36/80, ff. 9r–20r; Rawson, pp. 72–3, 78). For a full discussion of the siege, see J. Oates, 'The Last Siege on English Soil: Carlisle, December 1745', *Transactions of the Cumberland and Westmorland Archaeological and Antiquarian Society, New Series*, III, 2003, pp. 169–84.
68 Cumberland arrived in sight of Carlisle on 21 December. Bland and 300 of St George's Dragoons were positioned on the northern side of the city, Major Adams and 200 infantry stood in the suburbs near the south east. The sally port was guarded by Major Meriac and

as we were inform'd the place we were going to was fit (25r) neither for man nor beast to live in and so I marched on foot all that day which Rain'd continually in a very bad Country. When we came within 3 miles of Carlisle we turn'd off to the right hand in order to cross the River by Warwick Bridge which took us about 5 miles aboutt and that night as it continu'd raining very hard & began to grow Dark we halte'd at a little Village caled Crosbie within 2 miles of (26v) of Stanwicks where we lay all that night the men in very bad quarters & officers by the fire sides. Nixt day we had orders to be at Stanwick before day light as there was a rising ground we had to go over that was exposed to the fire from the Castle which they keep pritty constant [69] to that side the Duke lay on but it was represented to us to be of much greater danger to gett to the place than it actually was which made us take more caution in marching (26r) that there was need for. We got to Stanwicks Bank at about 8 o Clock of Christmas morning a wretched poor place to spend that time in & found Gen. St. Georges Dragoons [70] lying there & Blighs Foot had marched from thence that morning to go & joyn the Dukes army which was canton'd on the west side of the town as we came to supply their place. As soon as the men were all come up Gen Bland [71] who commanded on that side the River gave orders for (27v) the 4 youngest Compays to be quarter'd in 2 villages about half a mile distance & the other 4 cos to continue there & were to be reliev'd in their turns. This day Capt Stewarts Compy mounted the Guard being first upon command & at night Capt Tongues mounted a reserve Guard & nothing extraordinary hapn'd. That night orders were given by the Genl for neither officer nor soldier to go to bed but allways to be in readiness to turn out at a moments warning which (27r) orders were continud all the time we lay in that place & were strictly observ'd by our Regiment as they had no place to lye in but the Guard Rooms the other houses being all took up by the Dragoons before we came. Nixt day our Compy & Mason's mounted the two Guards the officers of the other two cos were to go round every hour of the night to see that their men were all alert & awake. This afternoon the Duke came around to our side of the River to reconoyter & went down by (28v) himself to view the castle & city which was the first time I had seen him. Our Compys were reliev'd in the morning by Capt Tongue & Stewart & we were orderd to do the same duty as they were on the day before about 12 o clock that night we were alarm'd & all out under arms

---

another 200 infantrymen. The remaining troops, mostly cavalry and Foot Guards, were cantoned a mile from Carlisle. According to Ray, the force initially numbered 4,000 men, later rising to 5,500. (TNA, SP36/78, f. 14r; Ray, p. 230).

69   There were 46 cannon found in the castle after the surrender, six pounders and guns of even lower calibre. They caused few casualties (one dead and four or five wounded), perhaps because there were so few trained gunners manning them. (TNA, SP36/80, ff. 26r, 104r; RA, CP, 8/113).

70   Later the 8th Horse. They had formerly being under Marshal Wade's command, but the latter had ordered them to ride in pursuit of the Jacobites. (Blaikie, *Itinerary*, p. 95).

71   Major General Humphrey Bland (c. 1686–1763), Quarter Master General, made Major General during the '45. (*ODNB*, 6, pp. 158–60).

the main & reserve Guard march'd down to the trenches which was rais'd by the sentry upon the end of the Bridge where there was a Guard continually kept of a Troop of Dragoons & a Detachment from our (28r) Reserve Guard of an officer & 25 men having seen severall people come over the walls & they had quite left off passing the word round the Garrison wch made us suspect that they intended making a sally that night. We stood under arms about an hour & fir'd a few shots off to lett them know we were in readiness to exercise them but they all kept quite so we orderd the men in again & sent a party to a ford below to see if there were any of them making their escape that way but they met wth non. (29v) Just at that time came in a waggon with 4 coarns from Genl Wades [72] army & in a little after they began playing them from the trenches this night they threw about 25 shells wch mostly fell either in the town or castle & brought a very hot fire upon the place yt the Trench Guard was kept in while I was going the visiting Rounds there they fir'd a round of Grape or Case Shott which fell very thick about us but no body was hurt as we were pritty (29r) well shelter'd by the Trenches. Upon Saturday morning about 8 o Clock the Duke open'd his Battery wch was Situated upon a Rising Gnd on the west side of the Castle & consisted of 6 18 pdr Cannon which he had from Whitehaven [73] their fire was return'd very briskly [74] from the castle from [*illegible*] & 3 Gun Battery which they Continud all this day very warmly & now & then they let a shot fly to ourside (30v) when our men appeard over curious in looking at them which they were very frequently being now growen quit Bold by no body being hurt. Our Coll Had a very narrow escape as he was going past the Guard that I was upon a Shot being fired from the 8 Gn Battery the Ball just mised him & broak a Tree that was hard by. This Night all our 4 Comps were upon Guard & the Caorns were thrown as formerly (30r) Sunday the Battery & Castle began to cannonade one another about day light & Continued it till dark when the Castle slackened very much in the heat of their firing as they were now quite bett from the 4 Gn Battery by the Dukes Cannon. This night 4 more 18 pdr Came up from Whitehaven to the Duke & when dark they began making a Battery for them some little nearer the Castle than the other which was Compleated nixt morning. I was all this night upon the Trench Guard. And (31v) as I march'd my Detachment down the Castle fired 4 Guns at the Caorns which were just then throwen but did no damage as we kept close in to the Fence &

---

72 Field Marshal George Wade (1673–1748), commander of the forces sent to Newcastle upon Tyne in October 1745. He was relieved of his command on 21 December 1745 by General John Huske. His command included ten coehorn mortars, which could lob grenades over fortress walls. Six were used at Culloden. (*ODNB*, 56, pp. 658–61; TNA, SP36/78, f. 15v).

73 The eighteen-pounder cannon arrived on 28 December. For a full discussion of these guns, see D. Hepburn and C. Richards, 'Documents Relating to the Transportation of Cannon from Whitehaven to Carlisle during the Jacobite Rebellion of 1745', *Transactions of the Cumberland and Westmorland Archaeological and Antiquarian Society, New Series*, 84 (1984), pp. 142–66.

74 According to James Miller, one of the garrison, 'we return'd this [i.e. cannon fire] pretty sharply considering our mettle being but small'. (J.H. Leslie, 'Diary of James Miller, 1745–1750', *The Journal of the Society for Army Historical Research*, III (1924), p. 209).

heard the Ball flye over us. These were the last shott that the Enemy fired being very quite all night & in the morning immediately after the first round from the Battery they hung out a white flagg to shew that they want'd a Conference with the Duke which they had accordingly [75] (31r) & firing was given over on both sides. This day was spent in sending of messages to & froe till it was night when all the foot with the Duke march'd into the City at the Irish Gate [76] & at same time Stewarts Compy of our Regiment & 60 Drags of St. Georges dismounted went & took possession of the Scotch Gate. [77] The city had surrenderd to the Duke upon no other Terms that leaving themselves at the King's mercy so that night a messenger was sent to London to know his pleasure. [78] (32v) Our 3 Coys that were still at Stanwick mounted Guard thatt night in 3 different places & the Trenches were filled up to have an easier communication with the Town. Nixt day nothing extraordinary hapned only the Duke entering the town at which time all the Guns in the Castle were fired. Orders were given by Genl Bland that non of the officers nor soldiers on our side should offer to cross the Bridge upon any Reason whatever which the men thought very hard as they (32r) were very desirous to gett into good Quarters & Curious to see the Highlanders. [79] Our 4 oldest Compys had been now upon duty for 6 Nights running without ever geting any rest or being reliev'd by the younger ones as was at first propos'd at which they made great complaints & indeed I must say they had Reason for it as they were now growing sick in great numbers & quite stupid for want of Rest. [80] However there was noe Redress for them (33v) This day at noon our Compay was order to mount the main Guard which went very ill down with us however we Resolved to make no Complt as we looked upon this to be the last Scene of our hardship Had not the town surrendered when it did this would have been a turn of much harder duty than itt was being a very easy one having nothing now to fear. As this was the time the Duke had fix'd upon to storm the Breach of the Castle which would (33r) have been by this time pritty wide. His designe was as I afterwards heard to have attacked itt with 800 foot by Detachment from all that were with

75 On 30 December, the garrison displayed a white flag and sent messages to try to negotiate a surrender. Cumberland's reply was 'All the terms his royal highness will or can grant to the rebel garrison of Carlisle are, that they shall not be put to the sword, but be reserved for the King's pleasure'. The terms were accepted, though Townley wished to fight on. However, the Jacobites' ammunition was almost exhausted. (TNA, SP36/78, ff. 280r, 282r; Blaikie, *Origins*, p. 193; RA, CP, 8/209).
76 Also known as Caldoe Gate. It is to the west of the city. (*The Gentleman's Magazine*, 15 (1745), p. 675).
77 Also known as Richard Gate. It is on the north east side of the city. (Ibid.)
78 Newcastle told Cumberland that he was allowed to treat with the rebels if he thought proper. (TNA, SP36/78, ff. 225r-226r.
79 Cumberland allowed General Bligh to take 400 Foot Guards, another 700 infantrymen and 120 cavalrymen to enter Carlisle, in order to secure the prisoners and to take any of their surplus arms and ammunition. Looting was forbidden on pain of strict punishment. (*The Gentleman's Magazine*, 16 (1746), pp. 21–2).
80 According to Ray 'We had very bad weather; so that the Army in general was very much fatigued'. Some died of small pox. (Ray, p. 241; R. Cumberland, *Memoirs* (London, Lackington, 1806), p. 57).

him so that our proprtion of it would have been abt 200. Butt thank God that it hapnend as it did else a good many lives would have been lost in the attempt. [81] Nixt morning the 1st of Jany we were all order'd to be under arms by 8 in the morning & marched off from (34v) Stanwick by 9 we expected to have haulted in Carlisle all that day but were disapointd as we marched in Review thro' the town past the Duke the officers all Saluted with their half pickes [82] as they past him & Coll Graham stood by & gave him a Character of us which I believe was fully as good as we deserv'd. He gave the Coll orders to march us directly for Liverpool & there waitt his further orders. So (34r) this night we reached Penrith. But an accident hapned me which I was afterwards very glad of as by it I had an opportunity of returning to Carle & there saw all the prisoners Castle & that were worth seeing. Capt Spencer had sent his servt the Day after the town surerender'd to Penrith for his own & my bagage which we had left there not to be troubled with it att the Siege but the people whose care it was in had sent it some days before (35v) to the Dukes quarts thinking it belong'd to the forces with him which the servant came up & informed us off upon the march about 2 miles out of town so I Returned back again & found the bagage & followed them to Penrith after I had diverted myself some time among the Prisoners but had a troublesome journy of it as the Old Horse I borrowd (my own being left at Penrith) grew tyred about half way (35r) to Penrith & obliged me to walk on foot the other half in the Dark. Nixt morning we marched from Penrith and gott into Kendall pritty soon considering the distance to be 20 long miles. From there we marched to Lancaster in a day. And nixt to Preston where the Coll thought propper to halt all Sunday as the four last days had been very hard upon the men but the weather was then too good to loose a day of it. At this time oth year we having [The Duke went through here past about 10 o Clock on his way to London[83]] (36v) had nothing but fine days from we left Carlisle. At Preston we found Ld Hallifax [84] & the Marq of Granby's Regim [85] two new ones but very good looking men which with the quarters taken for the 4 Troops of Ligonier's Horse [86] that had marched with us from Carle had so filled the town that our 4 oldest Compys were obliged to be quarterd in the little Villages near the town where they had very good intertainment. Monday the 6th Jany (36r) We made a short march to Ormskirk. And as Tuesday was the Post day at Liverpool the Coll went forward there & order'd the Regiment to houses

---

81 Cumberland earlier remarked to Newcastle that an assault would only 'expose ourselves to any considerable loss', later adding 'the strength of the town and castle, but especially the castle, which if the rebels had chose to have held out must have cost us some blood and much time'. (TNA, SP36/78, f. 15v; RA, CP, 9/13–14).

82 Officers carried half pikes or spontoons.

83 After the fall of Carlisle, Cumberland handed command to General Henry Hawley, and briefly returned to London. (R. Whitworth, *William Augustus, Duke of Cumberland* (Barnsley, Pen and Sword Books Ltd, 1993), p. 68).

84 Sir George Montagu-Dunk (1716–71), 2nd Earl of Halifax. He raised another of the 'New' Regiments. (Lewis, *Walpole Correspondence*, 30, p. 437).

85 John Manners (1721–70), M.P., Marquis of Granby. He raised another of the 'New' Regiments. (*ODNB*, 36, pp. 466–9).

86 See n. 52. (Ibid., p. 434).

till we heard from him as he was in great expectations of having the Dukes orders
to Continue the Regiment and if so he did not care to let them come into the Town
but as nothing came that day he sent orders for us to march into town nixt morning. So on Wednesday the 8th we returned to Liverpool. (37v) which unluckily
hapned to be a very Rainy day & disapoind us greatly in the appea we intended
to have made wch would have been to the best advantage as the men had all got
their arms & cloaths very clean but were now quite Rust & Durtied by the Rain.
We here mounted a Capts guard & had the men out under arms every other day
in the same manner as when from home which was done meerly to keep the men
together & in reading (37r) if any orders should come from the Duke about estab-
lishing the Regiment which the Coll wished for very earnestly as he was very
much grieved to think of Disbanding so good a Body of men at this time. However
after having waited for some orders from the Duke as he had told the Coll he
would let him hear from him at Carlisle & no answer coming to a letter the mayor
had wrote about takg the Regiment into the King's pay as the subscription
mony [87] (38v) was now almost spent & consequently we must either be Disbanded
or established immediatly. The Gentn of the town came to a Resolution (but not
with the Consent of the Coll who would fain have persuaded ym to continue the
Regiment some time longer) that if they heard nothing by Tuesdays Post they must
be disbanded as they say they must have had an answer to their letter if the King
had any thoughts of taking them into his pay & that it was a (38r) needless &
very great expense to keep the men lying here Idle & of no Service. So on Tuesday
the 14th of Jany no letter coming we were ordered to be all out under arms in the
Town field & there the Regiment being formed into a circle the Coll went about
along with the Mayor [88] &c made a Short Speech to every Compay leting them
know that they were now Disbanded & at their own Liberty to goe where they
pleased but desired that they would stay in town in case the Regiment should (39v)
be Raised again & that they would not inlist themselves in any other Regimt for
some time. After that each Company marched down to their Capts quarters & there
deliver'd up their arms & ammunition receive'd what pay was due to them & so
were Dismissed. [89] The three field officers stayed some days in town to see what
a little time would produce but no orders coming they all Returned to their
Respective posts as also did the Rest of the officers to their (39r) former different Employments in life. So here ends the History of the Liverpool Regimt. During
the time that I was engaged in this affair I cant say that I ever before spent any
time more agreeably and I am sure that most of the Gentlemen that were with us
will say the same with me. For though we frequently had a great dale of Fatigue
& trouble in our marches and other ways yet that was always made more than
amends for (40v) by the mirth & joy that we afterwards had when we got into
our Quarters & the Constant Harmony that we lived in wth one another. And I

87 See n. 6. With the ending of the subscription money, there would be no more pay for the
   men.
88 James Bromfield was Mayor, 1745–46. (Picton, *Municipal Records*, p. 109).
89 According to Picton, the men were dismissed on 15 January 1746. (Ibid., p. 108).

dare say most of the officers would have had a great dale of pleasure in continuing longer in that way of life if they had had an opportunity of doing it in the same Rank they were then in. But there was one thing which we all could not help looking upon as ungratefull & not good usage & (40r) that was the Governments taking so little notice of us as not answering the Mayors letter even after the Duke as we are certainly informed had given a very great character of us in London [90] & as we were the best New Regiment raised in the Kingdom upon the same occasion & the very only one that had been of any service till then. Yet was there 13 the New ones [91] established & we left out.

Finis.

Appendices

Appendix 1

A List of the Officers who Comanded the Eight Companys of Liverpool Blues
Coll Graham Lt Coll Gordon & Major Bendish Field Officers.
1st Capt Tongue Lieut Whittle En Sacheverell
2d Spencer Shairp Halsall
3d Mason Dunbar. Kenyon [92]
4th Stewart Strong. [93] Smith
5th Campbell Haliday. Lee
6th Weakly Armitage. [94] Strong
7th Heywood Heyes. Todd
8th Colquitt Farmer. Dugdale
Lieut Dunbar Adjutant
Lieut Whittle Quartermastr
Ensn Lee adjutant after Dunbar threw it up at Wiggan.

90 Cumberland told Bromfield on 29 November, 'I can't help taking notice to you how much I am pleased with the account Colonel Grimes [sic] gives of your regiment'. (Ibid., p. 113). After the Jacobites had left England, there was little need for the volunteer regiments to be kept in service. Most were dismissed in January.
91 Plans were afoot by fifteen noblemen in late September 1745 to raise regiments against the rebellion. Apart from those mentioned, the others were the Dukes of Devonshire, Bedford, Montagu, Rutland and Bolton, and Lords Harcourt, Falmouth, Berkeley, Herbert, Edgecumbe, Ancaster and Derby. However, only a few were actually formed. They were to number 273 cavalrymen or 814 infantrymen. (Lewis, *Walpole Correspondence*, 19, p. 128).
92 J. Kenyon, member of the Liverpool Ugly Face Club. (Howell, p. 65).
93 Matthew Strong (d.c. 1774), merchant; Mayor of Liverpool, 1768–69; member of the Ugly Face Club. (Higham, p. 114; Irvine, *Wills at Chester, 1761–1780*, II, R.S.L.C., 38 (1899), p. 63; Howell, p. 65).
94 W. Armitage, member of the Liverpool Ugly Face Club. (Howell, p. 65).

Appendix 2

To stuff a Horse Foot if suspected to be prick'd

Take one Ounce of Turpentine, one ounce of Hogs Lard, half one ounce of Rosin half a gill of Train oil and a quarter of one ounce of Bees Wax.

For a Cold

Take a pinte of milk and Boill three Cloves of Garlick in it till the milk is made yellow by the Garlick. Before it is quit cold mix in it a spoon full of Honey and a spoon full of Sallad Oyle and give it in a horn to the Horse.

He must fast three hours before he get this Drink and of Long after and must have no water in the morning his water must be warmed for him at night for the garlick will make him sweat. This Drink must be given For days running if the could be Bad. It cannot hurt your Horse if hes kept warm.

For the Grouse

Half a Pound of Rye
Flour a Pint of Crab Vinegar
Half a Pound of Hogs lard
Two penny worth of Ran Turpentine

Put these in a clean Pot and both them together. Then spread it on a piece of Gray paper and lay it to the horses heels Binding them over with a lin ring cloth for 48 hours keeping his legs from water.

THE WRITINGS OF THE CRAGG FAMILY OF WYRESDALE

Edited by Katrina Navickas

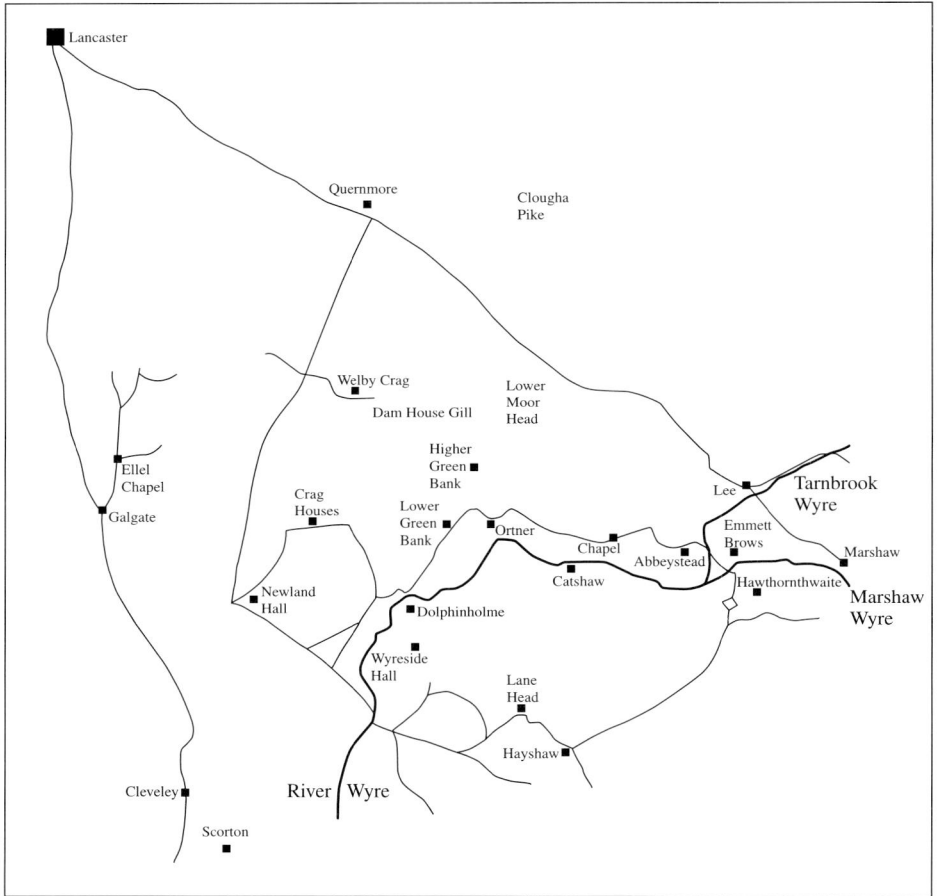

Map of Over Wyresdale based on Yates's Map of Lancashire, 1786.

INTRODUCTION

The Craggs were a yeoman family who lived in Over Wyresdale, Lancaster parish, from at least the late sixteenth century. They were prolific writers about their own lives and the events affecting their region. As Quakers, their historicism was part of a natural desire to emulate George Fox and his successors, who inspired journal-writing as a means of examining one's inner light and of providing an example to future generations. Yet their memorandum book was also a response to the dramatic political events which directly involved their region during the eighteenth century, together with the social and economic changes engendered by industrialisation in the North West of England. The Glorious Revolution of 1688 and the Jacobite rebellions of 1715 and 1745 placed before every family and individual a distinct choice of political allegiance: either for or against the monarchy as sanctioned by parliament. This choice could even be translated locally to one of being for or against one's own neighbours. Tensions eased in the latter half of the century, but in the closing decade, the French Revolution and the influence of the widely-distributed *Rights of Man* by Thomas Paine raised the spectre of a similar choice for new generations within the same families. What survives of the Cragg family's writings is, in part, testimony to how national events and ideologies were important even to otherwise unremarkable provincial families and shaped their choices of allegiance and how they lived their lives.

Context and Composition of the Writings

The two protagonists of the Cragg family memorandum book are Timothy Cragg (1736–1828), of Greenbank in Over Wyresdale, and his son David (1769–1835). It appears that they were the principal instigators of the project to record the history of their family, although the differing tones and styles of the entries in the memorandum book suggest that other members of the family were involved.[1] It was not the only piece of hagiography and local history on which the Craggs worked. In 1797, David Cragg transcribed 'The Life of Timothy Cragg of the Chappelhouse in Wyersdale'. This is a moving conversion narrative written by his great-grandfather in the late seventeenth century, which also includes information on provincial attitudes towards the Duke of Monmouth's rebellion.[2] Finally, David compiled his own diary, which was published in 1977 by G. Fandrey, a Canadian descendant. The latter also noted that in 1803, David Cragg collected material on a book he intended to write on the history of Wyresdale.[3] Parts of this probably form part of the early pages of the memorandum book.

---

1 LCRO, DDX 760/1, 'Cragg family memorandum book'. For a further discussion of the debate over the authorship of the manuscript and its political content, see K. Navickas, 'The Cragg Memorandum Book: Society, Politics and Religion in North Lancashire in the 1790s', *Northern History*, XLII:1 (March 2005), pp. 151–62.
2 LCRO, LG3/CRAG, 'The Life of Timothy Cragg of the Chappelhouse in Wyersdale' [typescript].
3 G. Fandrey, *The Craggs of Greenbank* (Saskatchewan, 1977).

In the context of Quaker hagiography, it is perhaps curious why the family did not publish their history themselves or that their friends did not produce a biographical account, as many other Friends did.[4] Indeed, such biographies were included in a list of the Craggs' reading in July 1787. In part, this omission most likely had its causes in the political situation of repression of seditious material in the 1790s. After criticising the start of the war on 9 February 1793, one of Timothy's sons (unspecified in the memorandum book) wrote that his father had commanded him 'to write nothing about the war or Thomas Paine or politics of any sort, for if anybody saw what I have already written I should be tried for libel and perhaps hanged'. He thus vowed to himself that he would burn the diary 'if any disturbance should take place'. The diary's survival indicates that their anxiety about being arrested in rural north Lancashire was psychological rather than physical. The Craggs' fears were engendered by awareness of the repression of radicals nationally, especially the well-publicised attack on Joseph Priestley and the royal proclamations against seditious writings of May and December 1792. They did not face the more direct threats of suppression which the magistrates in the industrialising towns of south Lancashire inflicted upon local radicals, although the Craggs appear to have been silent witnesses to the 'Church and King' burning of an effigy of Thomas Paine by a working-class crowd in Dolphinholme on New Year's Day 1793. They may have complied or acquiesced in the event on this occasion to avoid the crowd turning against them.[5]

The Craggs' outward reputation was therefore more likely to have been religious than political. As Quakers they were conspicuous, but there may have been less prejudice than in other places because of the high proportion of Friends in the region. Nevertheless, their religious identity was still identified with 'the other' during the economic strains of the war. The Craggs, amongst other Quakers, were involved in the grain trade. In 1800, they commented about Richard Cragg carting meal at night for fear of mobs at Lancaster and elsewhere: 'Being a Badger now is somewhat a dangerous trade'. Conspiracy theories abounded about Quakers forestalling grain during the shortages, and it appears that the Craggs feared participants in food riots more than the Church-and-King mobs in this period.[6]

Personal reasons dictated why David Cragg did not publish a version of his own diary. He certainly intended to leave some record for posterity. According to Fandrey, in 1805 David spent much time editing the second book of the 'history of myself.' With an editor's over-critical eye, he 'read over much of his writing

---

4   See for example, J. D. Marshall, ed., *The Autobiography of William Stout of Lancaster, 1665–1752* (Chetham Society, Third Series, 14, 1967); J.S. Harford, *An Account of the Latter Days of Richard Vickris Pryor* (Bristol, ?1810). On the other hand, the extensive diary of the Craggs' relation, John Kelsall (1683–1743), also remained unpublished; the ms. is now held at the Library of the Society of Friends, London.

5   The memorandum book charts the progress of Dolphinholme worsted mill and its workers. See C. Aspin, *The Water Spinners* (Helmshore, Helmshore Local History Society, 2003), pp. 305–12, for a history of the mill; also *The Family Records of Benjamin Shaw, Mechanic of Dent, Dolphinholme and Preston, 1772–1841*, ed. A. G. Crosby, R.S.L.C., cxxx (1991).

6   For the history of food riots and attitudes towards forestalling, see A. Booth, 'Food Riots in the North West of England, 1790–1801', *Past and Present*, 77 (1977), pp. 84–107.

and of upwards of seven hundred sheets, he destroyed two or three hundred of them'. This was in part a cathartic process to rid himself of memories of a failed courting; on 29 March he wrote:

> My sentiments at that time were in some respects very different to what they are now. At that time I was deeply engaged in my mind concerning Mary Warbrick.[7]

David's diary, as published by his descendant, contrasts strikingly with the memorandum book. It remains highly personal, concerned with internal conflicts within the Cragg family, particularly concerning David's relationship with Molly Pye, the servant daughter of a Methodist preacher. It speaks little of politics or current affairs but charts in detail the social and emotional pressures placed upon some Quakers who followed their hearts rather than the will of their parents and religion. The personal challenges facing David have been discussed in Fandrey's edition of the diary and therefore will not be elucidated further here.

What remains in Lancashire County Record Office are therefore mere fragments of what was originally a much larger history of the Cragg family, most of which was lost by self-editing or perhaps transported over to Canada, where David Cragg settled in the 1830s.[8] A copy of the memorandum book rather than the original exists in the record office. This copy was seemingly transcribed in the later nineteenth century and therefore cannot be regarded as complete or entirely accurate. Indeed, it may have substituted the Quaker practice of numbering of months for the Julian calendar. Nevertheless, this brief glimpse into the political views and analyses of a yeoman family from a provincial corner of England is highly valuable to the historian. The strength of radical feeling expressed in most of the political comments is striking and highly significant. E.P. Thompson lauded how Paine's *Rights of Man* reached and inspired the handloom weavers and artisans in industrialising towns.[9] The memorandum book demonstrates that the new radical ideas in print reached even relatively isolated yeoman families in the most innocuous rural areas distant from urban intellectual debate. It also sheds light on how republican notions infused into a longer tradition within a religious sect which had suffered two centuries of being persecuted and discriminated against. The Quakers' essential pacifism reacted to Paine in a unique way. The Craggs' attitudes towards the war, oaths and conscription into the militia were an integral product of their religion, but the new circumstances of the French Revolution and the egalitarian teachings of Paine brought their deep-held beliefs into a new perspective. Certainly only a minority of Quakers were radical in their politics in this period, but the Craggs' response is significant in their analyses of events and at least one member of the family's wish to record their beliefs.

---

7 Fandrey, *Craggs of Greenbank*, p. 34.
8 Ibid.
9 E. P. Thompson, *The Making of the English Working* Class, new edition (Harmondsworth, Penguin, 1968).

Genealogical Table*

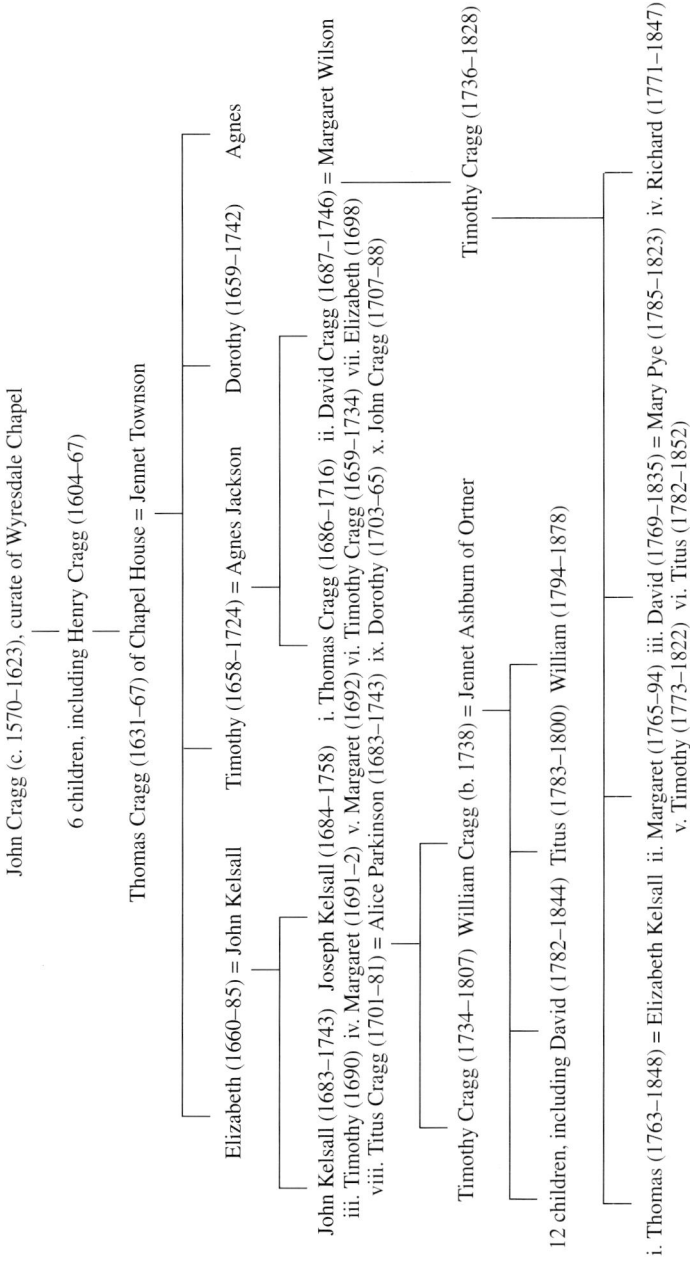

John Cragg (c. 1570–1623), curate of Wyresdale Chapel

6 children, including Henry Cragg (1604–67)

Thomas Cragg (1631–67) of Chapel House = Jennet Townson

Elizabeth (1660–85) = John Kelsall   Timothy (1658–1724) = Agnes Jackson   Dorothy (1659–1742)   Agnes

John Kelsall (1683–1743) Joseph Kelsall (1684–1758)   i. Thomas Cragg (1686–1716) ii. David Cragg (1687–1746) = Margaret Wilson
iii. Timothy (1690) iv. Margaret (1691–2) v. Margaret (1692) vi. Timothy Cragg (1659–1734) vii. Elizabeth (1698)
viii. Titus Cragg (1701–81) = Alice Parkinson (1683–1743) ix. Dorothy (1703–65) x. John Cragg (1707–88)

Timothy Cragg (1736–1828)

Timothy Cragg (1734–1807) William Cragg (b. 1738) = Jennet Ashburn of Ortner

12 children, including David (1782–1844) Titus (1783–1800) William (1794–1878)

i. Thomas (1763–1848) = Elizabeth Kelsall ii. Margaret (1765–94) iii. David (1769–1835) = Mary Pye (1785–1823) iv. Richard (1771–1847)
v. Timothy (1773–1822) vi. Titus (1782–1852)

* Lancashire County Record Office, FRL 2/1/9/1, Wyresdale Monthly Meeting record of births; MF 1/49, Lancaster Monthly Meeting record of burials; 'Cragg Family Register Report 2004', unpublished mss compiled by Mr John Harris.

The Cragg Family and Politics

The Cragg family's interests were based on a small estate which they gradually built up through renting plots from their neighbours. The Friends Meeting minutes and the Lancaster poll book of 1802 classed Timothy Cragg (1736–1828) as a yeoman, with his sons as husbandmen.[10] To be classed as a yeoman in north Lancashire was a mark of social recognition as much as relative wealth. It implied sufficient economic independence, not necessarily owning many acres but farming land with a substantial rental value and having a measure of social status within the local community.[11] Their wills illustrate how the estate in Greenbank built up through the years was kept in the family. Timothy left his eldest son the estate and provided his other sons with hundreds of pounds each; an old 'ark' in a room over the kitchen was passed down as an heirloom.[12] The family did well from the high agricultural prices of the French and Napoleonic Wars. Fandrey states that David was unable to leave home in 1801 because his father was becoming overwhelmed with the work on the farm. David Cragg's diary recorded in 1804 that his father rented a farm in Greenbank vaccary for his brother Thomas after his marriage at the yearly rent of fifty-two pounds.[13] Timothy was able to help another of David's brothers to buy his own farm at Welby Crag (about four miles away from Ortner) in the same year. In 1811, David Cragg was paying interest on a mortgage worth £600 for his own estate at Greenbank.[14] Their life as yeomen therefore gave them a sense of independence and identification with the land.

The period covered by the manuscripts was one of great political and religious upheaval for most provincial inhabitants. The history of Lancashire Quakers during the first phase of Jacobitism has been well covered by N. Morgan.[15] He demonstrates how oath-taking was a central issue to Quakers. He moreover emphasises how Friends' loyalty to the political establishment deepened through the succession crisis, culminating in genuine commitment to the Hanoverians. William Stout of Lancaster, for example, wrote that it 'gave great satisfaction to all well wishers of the nation's true interest' when the new King George declared his support for the 1689 Toleration Act.[16] Quakers then spent the eighteenth century in relatively well-organised but ultimately unsuccessful campaigns against oaths, tithes and taxation. These issues indeed form a substantial part of the memorandum book's comments on and criticisms of the interference of Parliament and government in provincial affairs.

---

10 LCRO, QDL/1798/LS/47, Over Wyresdale Land Tax Return, 1798; information from the Friends' Registers supplied by Society of Friends Library, London; *Lancaster Electioneering Papers* (Lancaster, 1802).
11 D. E. Ginter, 'Measuring the Decline of the Small Landowner', in B.A. Holderness and M. Turner, *Land, Labour and Agriculture, 1700–1920* (London, Hambledon, 1990), pp. 36–7.
12 LCRO, WRW A 1828, will of Timothy Cragg, yeoman of Greenbank in Over Wyresdale.
13 Fandrey, *Craggs of Greenbank*, p. 37.
14 Ibid., p. 50.
15 N. Morgan, *Lancashire Quakers and the Establishment, 1660–1730* (Halifax, Ryburn, 1993).
16 Ibid., p. 74.

The account of the life of Timothy Cragg (1658–1724) therefore presents a complement to Morgan's conclusions. The Cragg memorandum book is furthermore a contrast and continuation in the longer timespan, after toleration and the gradual easing of prejudice against Friends. The life is mainly a conversion narrative, written with the purpose of inspiring the 'fear of God' into his descendants. Timothy was churchwarden of Wyresdale, but realised his principles better accorded with the Friends. This affected another significant part of his life, his soldiering. He joined James II's militia, but his increasing hatred of the oath and his pacifism led to his refusal to take up arms in the Lancaster militia in response to the arrival of William of Orange. Significantly, he suggested that those who enrolled in the militia, swore the oath of allegiance or appeared as supporters of James II, in fact shared secret allegiance to the invading Duke of Monmouth: 'and yet our hearts was for the Duke'. Petrie argued that support received by Monmouth across the country demonstrated that many Dissenters were prepared to oppose James's plans for toleration if they had to share it with Roman Catholics. Some also objected to plans to raise the numbers of the standing army in order to free the Crown from its dependence on Whig magnates in the militia.[17] This could have been a cover for suspicion that the militia was a tool of the Tories.

The life of Timothy Cragg was a significant part of the Cragg family's identity, both during his lifetime and for his descendants in the 1790s.[18] It is therefore interesting to compare Timothy's leanings towards the rebel Monmouth and the radicalism in the Cragg memorandum book. Initially, the book's comments about George III are neutral. After the royal proclamation on seditious writings of May 1792, however, the tone changes. The King from then on is continually referred to as a despotic tyrant. This was not the loyalty to the Hanoverians that Timothy Cragg might have professed along with all of Morgan's loyal Quakers. The writer of the radical comments in the memorandum book was imbued with the republican spirit of Thomas Paine and evoked the more established language of eighteenth-century constitutionalist radicalism as espoused by John Wilkes and Major Cartwright.[19]

This shift of perceptions of the British monarchy perhaps implies that the writer of the radical comments felt a sense of affinity to some elements of Jacobitism. The popular response to Jacobitism, positive or negative, entailed choices relating to loyalties, established beliefs and people's view of their place within the larger political nation. The radical Cragg could have identified with these challenges in the new circumstances of the 1790s. The deep effect of the rebel armies in those areas they passed through is illustrated by the fact that most of the early entries in the memorandum book are retrospective notes about Lancaster and Preston in 1715. Cragg mentioned the efforts of the Earl of Derwentwater. The Earl's foe

17 C. Petrie, *The Jacobite Movement, the First Phase, 1688–1716*, revised and enlarged edition (London, Eyre & Spottiswoode, 1948), pp. 56, 60.
18 D. Rooksby, *The Quakers in North-West England, Part 3: And Sometime Upon the Hills* (Colwyn Bay, Rooksby, 1998), p. 87.
19 See H.T. Dickinson, *The Politics of the People in Eighteenth Century Britain* (Basingstoke, Macmillan, 1994).

in Lancashire was Sir Henry Hoghton, who clearly believed that the sympathies of the local inhabitants were questionable: 'We have some friends but few in comparison to those against us...As to our county, our enemys are as strong as then, and I know of no converts to be depended on'.[20] David Cragg's own father (b. 1736) was too young to remember both Jacobite rebellions, but his great-uncle, Titus (1701–81), may have recounted his knowledge of the events to his younger relatives. It is interesting to note, however, that the memorandum book ceases its history of the Lancaster region after the first Jacobite rebellion and only restarts with more personal recollections from 1781. Perhaps memories of 1745 were too fresh or were amongst material which David destroyed as unsatisfactory.

It is striking that the North West in general and certain towns in Lancashire in particular had a propensity to welcome both Jacobitism and Jacobinism. The Jacobites attempted to find shelter and defence among the inhabitants of Preston, Liverpool and Manchester.[21] The survival of Jacobite celebrations in these towns, particularly 'Oak Apple Day' on 29 May, together with a strong non-juring core in Manchester Collegiate Church, suggest that Jacobitism had a resonant legacy among the discontented in Lancashire. The immediate response among the local inhabitants in the face of conquest and invasion, however, both in 1715 and 1745, was at the most acquiescent. Attraction to the cause of the Young Pretender remained more cultural than military. Some of these pro-Jacobite places became renowned for radical circles in the 1790s or United Englishmen cells with links to the United Irishmen during the Irish agitation of 1798–1801.[22] There are no direct correlations, however: a visit by the Pretender's army was certainly not a guarantee of radicalism later in the century, and other towns untouched by Jacobite influence developed radical reputations. The welcome given to the Pretender in Manchester came from the Fellows of the High Anglican and Tory Collegiate Church, members of which were prominent in repressing radicals in the 1790s. Nevertheless, some inchoate connection existed: it was less direct and owed more to a sense of personal, political or regional independence from both the King and the interference of Parliament expressed by the northern provinces. Jacobitism as an ideology was never fixed or monolithic. Despite its close association with Tory reactionism, P. Monod has argued that Jacobitism could adopt 'Whiggish' or Country attitudes. It altered its constitutional position to allow popular resistance to oppression, imitating Whig contractualism and thereby leaving a legacy to radicalism.[23] The Cragg memorandum book illustrates one result of the legacy of independence represented by Jacobitism's shadow over the radicals of the 1790s.

20 D. Hunt, *A History of Walton-le-Dale and Bamber Bridge* (Lancaster, Carnegie, 1997), p.66; LCRO, DDHo 475.
21 See *Beppy Byrom's Diary, an Eye-Witness Account of Bonnie Prince Charlie in Manchester*, ed. W. H. Thomson (Manchester, 1954).
22 See M. Elliott, *Partners in Revolution, the United Irishmen and France* (New Haven, Yale U.P., 1982).
23 P. Monod, *Jacobitism and the English People, 1688–1788* (Cambridge, Cambridge U.P., 1989), p. 42.

Furthermore, English Jacobitism and Jacobin radicalism were more than political stances: they were deeply permeated with local identity. The defence of Preston in 1715 involved a defence or indeed re-definition of the civic identity of the town as well as a revolt against the Hanoverian forces.[24] Timothy Cragg's life displayed little sense of geographical identity, but the memorandum book expressed a strong sense of connection with the region, even more than any adherence to a class. Local identity was infused by the Craggs' presence of over a hundred years in Over Wyresdale, generations working the land as yeoman farmers and being intimately involved in local affairs. Their regular trips to Lancaster market and Meeting House gave them a deep attachment to the wider region, while their involvement in Quakerism gave them national and international perspectives. Personally, they felt themselves to be independent yeomen, battling with ideology propagated by loyalists in Parliament; in their private musings and in public, challenging the various assessed taxes and the militia ballot imposed on the population during the war.

The Craggs' religious faith was also an integral part of their identity as it was for Lancaster and its surrounding rural areas. The Craggs were regular attenders at Wyresdale Preparatory Meeting. In the first half of 1801, David and his brother Thomas Cragg were appointed by the Preparatory Meeting on separate occasions to attend the Monthly Meeting at Lancaster.[25] Wyresdale Meeting House was built on a farm off Abbeystead Lane around 1710; a school was established there by Joseph Kelsall in 1800.[26] Quakerism was the predominant faith in the area (until Methodism spread amongst the artisans), such as in the colony on Emmett's or Emmotts, a remote hamlet on a hill overlooking Abbeystead and in which community David was to find his future wife. David commented in January 1796 about his father and two other Quakers being able to serve as jurymen after affirming rather than taking an oath. The Affirmation Acts of 1696, 1714 and 1722 prevented Quakers from using a form of words other than the required oaths to serve on juries or hold any government office. Yet his surprise perhaps underestimates Quaker influence in local government in Lancaster and its neighbouring townships. In the early eighteenth century William Stout, amongst other Quakers, acted as assessor and collector of the land and window taxes. Cragg's observation, however, indicates how toleration was finally being achieved. Several Quakers served as burgesses for the commonalty.[27] Many Wyresdale Friends, including David and his father, were freemen of Lancaster.

This local prominence had much to do with their success in business. Quakers were at the helm of commercial quarrying and hatting that came to the fore in north Lancashire.[28] Moor Head estate in Over Wyresdale consisted of several tenements occupied in the early eighteenth century by Quaker families involved in

24 Hunt, *A History of Walton-le-Dale*, p. 65.
25 LCRO, FRL 7/1/1/1, Wyresdale Preparative meeting book, 1801.
26 Rooksby, *And Sometime Upon the Hills*, p. 86.
27 Morgan, *Lancashire Quakers and the Establishment*, pp. 39–40.
28 D. H. Pratt, *English Quakers and the First Industrial Revolution* (New York, Garland, 1985), p. 82.

the hatting trade. Trading connections, often through the far-reaching but close-knit Quaker community, linked the most rural parts with the towns and with London. John Moore, for example, a Quaker who had family connections with Wyresdale and Quernmore, worked in London in 1802. From 1806 he managed a new workshop in the small village of Wray near Hornby for Christys, the London hat manufacturing firm. The village consequently established itself as a hatting colony.[29] Some Quakers from north Lancashire moved away from their yeoman roots and became prominent in commerce and finance in Lancaster, Liverpool and Manchester. Thomas and John Hodgson established the first cotton mills in Caton and made their fortunes by speculating in trade, including West African slavery, operating initially from Lancaster but subsequently from Liverpool.[30] The Quakers who remained yeomen maintained a strong family presence in the region. The same names occurred repeatedly in the Wyresdale Meeting minutes, particularly the Kelsalls and the Dillworths. Other Dillworths were influential citizens of Lancaster and Yealand Conyers, whose numerous daughters married into Quaker families in Lancaster, Kendal, Settle and Leeds.[31] These networks of connections illustrate how even rural areas had wider economic links and also the pan-regional identity and community that Quakers shared with Westmorland and the West Riding.

The regional and international religious connections of the Craggs, together with their interest in national politics, are balanced in the memorandum book with the detailed minutiae of parochial life in Wyresdale. The 'tyranny' of John Fenton Cawthorne in his dealings with his tenants paralleled in Cragg's mind the 'despotism' of George III. The devastating effects of floods upon both the agriculture and the industry of the district are recounted at length. The French wars and militia conscription renewed local tensions, channelling the 'fiscal-military state' from a national into a very parochial sphere. The litany of deaths of local individuals and their children, known to all, were as important to record in Cragg's belief as the more anonymous victims of the war he opposed. This was a deliberate history of the region, as influenced by national events.

The two manuscripts thus provide personal perspectives on the political and religious currents shaping north Lancashire in the late seventeenth and the eighteenth centuries. They demonstrate that even in seemingly remote areas, otherwise innocuous inhabitants had serious choices to make about allegiance and the nature of loyalty. They show how ingrained Quakerism became in the identity and economy of Lancaster and its district, and how these bonds helped sustain Friends through the persecutions and prejudices of the period. The memorandum book also gives vital indications of the effects of two of the forces sending shockwaves throughout the region in the 1790s: industrialisation and Paine's *Rights of Man.*

---

29 Ibid., p. 111.
30 M. Winstanley, ed., *Rural Industries of the Lune Valley* (Lancaster, Centre for North-West Regional Studies, University of Lancaster, 2000), p. 7.
31 D. Abbatt, *Quaker Annals of Preston and the Fylde, 1653–1900* (London, Headley, 1931), pp. 45–6.

Ultimately, they illustrate how all British inhabitants were able to draw upon concentric circles of identities in the later eighteenth century. A sense of British identity was often tempered or indeed shaped by smaller adherences to locality and region, and by wider connections of religion or class.

Acknowledgements

I am indebted to Mr John Harris of Guildford, for sending me his 'Cragg Family Register Report 2004', and photographs of Wyresdale. I also wish to thank: Lancashire County Record Office, Preston; the Society of Friends Library, London, for sending me additional genealogical information; and Brenda Pedersen of Ontario, Canada, a distant descendant of the Craggs.

KATRINA NAVICKAS 2005

'The Life of Timothy Cragg of the Chappelhouse in Wyersdale written by himself'- transcribed from the original mss by his great grandson David Cragg in 1797' – transcribed by Timothy E Cragg of Greenbank Canada, grandson of the above mentioned Timothy Cragg in 1886[1]:

I was born, at Chappelhouse, in Wyresdale, and was son of Thomas and Jennet, on 2nd day of the 10th month 1658. My parents was of the Protestant proffession and I was educated in the same by them. My great grandfather, John Cragg, came out of some part of Cumberland and was one called a clerke, being one that did the office of a Priest, according as it was practiced at that day and time. My mother's maiden name was Townson, of the Townsons of the Morehead, which Townsons came from Greenbank. My father died when I was about 9 years of age, or something past. My mother married again, as I take it, when I was something past 12 years of age. I was, my age considered, most desperately against her marriage, for he who was her husband, was a sort of rough man and one called a Quaker and that was all across to me.

But now, to look back into my early days, I can remember well, both before my father died and after his decease, that my mother was very carefull of me, and the rest of her children, that we should live in the fear of God, and that we should not swear, nor lye, nor be wild, nor talk idly; and I can remember that when the great plague was in London, and I heard people tell worrowful [*sic*] stories of it, I being then somewhat short of 7 years of age, and had some little scholership. To the best of my memory, we had a book called 'Crums of Comfort', which had a prayer in it that was to be read in the time of a pestelance, I suppose so ordered by the Church of England, for it is many a year since I saw it – to wit: the said book. I was at that time so concerned for the people at London that, as I remember, I read that prayer over many a time. But O, as I grew in years I grew in wildness, and sometimes when I had gone whistling or singing on my way, I had sometimes met with reproof in my bossom. As I grew elder I fell into company – with those that spent the first days in the afternoon with playing at penny pitch, or with shooting with bows and arrows, in the winter evenings with playing at cards sometimes all or most part of the night long, altho' my useing these games was more for sport than money, but besure an idle cause of life it was; and sometimes we met at the ale house and ranted and sung there, alas! Not thinking of our last end and tho' I was preserved out of swearing, yet in my young days I had an ill property of cursing things that grieved me. I was wonderfully preserved from having any unlawful doings with women and when I have taken a view of my past life, I have wondered and admired that I was so preserved clear in that matter, considering the temptation and opertunities I had to have acted in that kind of wickedness. I must say this was altogether a mercy, and I have great cause to

---

1 Lancashire County Record Office, G3, 'Life of Timothy Cragg'; original spellings and grammar are retained.

be truly thankfull to the Lord for the same. One thing I think not to omit, and that is tobbaco. At 22 I may say I was reproved about smokeing of it in the senate of my bossom many a time, and several years, but it being used by my companions, and I had got a custom of it, it was a hard thing to leave it, tho' I met with an abundance of exercise about it. At last I would and did give up the using it extravigently and used but a little of it every day – sometimes smokeing, sometimes chewing; but after a time in a great measure I was forced to give up that too. I ought not to be unthankfull that there was so long a day of mercy holden out to me, tho' by the way of judgment; for if judgment had not been poured down upon me, I believe I had not left that extravigent use of smokeing and chewing tobacco, and many other beloved lusts besides that. Yet I think tobacco may be lawfully taken as a physick. But to return. About the 26th year of my life I married with Agness Jackson, daughter of Peter of Hathornthwaite, who was of the Jacksons of Hathornthwaite. Her mother's maiden name was Croft, of the Crofts of Tummore in Littledale, and through mercy we have thus far lived a loveing life together, for which my soul has cause to praise the name of the Lord. Tho' we met with exercise, we having eleven children together, and of several of those children my wife was, as we thought, like to lose her life. We had seven sons and four daughters. Two of those sons was born dead, and one of the daughters died when about thirteen weeks of age. My eldest son Thomas lived till he was thirty years and three months old, the rest of them, at the writing hereof, being through mercy alive. But, to return again and take a view of my life past, about when I was twenty-two years of age I was put on for a trainband soldier, or one of the militia, which certainly led me into more jollity, jokeing, drinking and such like idleness and we met to be trained yearly for some years, and an abundance of idleness there was to be seen and heard. Tho' through mercy I was perservered from swearing, I heard abundance of it. The same year I was married. King James the 2nd then ruling, him that was called the Duke of Monmouth, came into this nation, into the southern part of it, and got a considerable army together, and then was the militia called up to meet at Lancaster, and I being one must of, for there was at that time no hireling or getting of for me, though I endeavoured of it, but in vain. But the thing that I most feared came upon me at that time, and that was the takeing the Oathes of Alegence and Supremacy, as they were then called; for I can remember yet, tho' it may be many years since, when the greater sort of officers said to this effect, 'now lads, for your oaths'. It struck to my heart like a dart. O! then I was strangly down [*sic*]; but was so cowardly that I did not stand to deny taking the oaths, nor any man in the whole regiment that I heard of, but one, and he was of our company, that I heard or can remember of. And yet our hearts was for the Duke; for when the news came that the Duke was taken, there was but a poor shout, for though we were so slavish to swear, yet we could not many of us be so hipocritical as to shout when the poor man was taken and his army routed. The takeing any oath was sometimes by me shunned, when I could well do it, it was so against me; I was sometimes so slaveish to taken an oath. Then this was about Monmouth being over, there passed in about two years, and I was put in for a church warden, as they are called. And in that year, which was the year 1687, I came to be convinced of many things, and one thing I think here to mention and it was thus: we had about that time many workmen, both wrights and masons, and some others which were employed in building, and they and were many of us young people, and a light airy course of life we led, some telling great stories and others laughing at them. I was at that time struck in my mind that that course of life we led was not right, and often in that year's being a warden, was amongst the priests, and I saw so much jarring and quarrelling when they met with one another, and the covetousness of some of them, that it set me against them. Neither was I satisfied with their formality in their worship, and sometimes I went to the Presbyterians to hear them; but it was not very often. But to go on. When I should have gone to the Bishop's court to be sworn at going into the office above mentioned, I went not and so was not sworn at going into the office, and when I went out at the year's end, I deny to swear in the open court, and the register he threatened me, because I would not swear, and there was two priests there. One of them would have prevailed me to have sworn. I told them of that scripture in Matthew about swearing; but one of the priests said it was spoke about vain swearing. But to that I could not agree.

I was likewise strangely alarmed about carding. One night I being at a neighbour's house carding, as I remember, for apples, and a considerable number of people playing, it happened that the wind rose very terrible, and it rained extremely; and I was struck with the thought, that if the house should be blown down upon our heads, what would become of our souls – or to this effect. So away out of the house I went home and soundly wet; but as I remember, I never carded more. I was convinced of several things that I was addicted to before I left the Church of England, and I may say I was one that was loth to bend, and was as I any word it, [*sic*] driven out by inward judgements, for there was a cross to be taken up. And tho' I had a loving wife, yet it was a cross to her for me to become a quaker, and she had then her father and one unkle living and one unkle dead – which in his time had been a famous preacher, and put forth two books. And for me to become a Quaker, was much against my wife's relations. Then I begun to frequent meetings of the people called Quakers, which was in the year 1688, for before that time I had been but a few meetings. A little after came the priest of the parish to discourse me, whose name was James Fenton, and abundance of discourse we had about swearing, baptising infants, abuses in bishops courts, and such like things; but when he saw he could not pervaile on me to bring me back, he was ever after very bitter against me. That same year came in the Prince of Orange and I, being a trainband soldier, must go, for the militia was called up to meet at Lancaster. So to the head of the company I went, to which I formally belonged; but did not put on either the red coat or took with me any arms. And when they called the list I appeared, and was not free to carry arms any longer – and so was freed just there and then. But as I had been baited as I may say with Fenton and some other priests, so at that time it was my lot to be discourced with soldiers, for I had been a merry blade amongst them and they were loth to part with me. And abundance of discource I was fors't to have with both relations and neighbours. But all these were but small matters to me in comparison of inward exercises I met with. This is certainly true, which I think here to write, that the weights and burdens I have at times met with hath been such that when it was evening I could have wish't for morning, and would needs be perswaided many a time, that no man's lot was like mine, nor never man did tread those steps that I trod. Alas! I am perswaided disobediance was the cause of these things – for want of giving up freely. Things was so with me that I have thought I could have been willing, if it were lawfull to have desired such a thing, tho' I had a loving wife and children, to have been in the farrest part of China, in my working clothes and clogs, so that the burdens and sorrows I lay under, might have been removed and that I might have been freed of those terrors and horrors that seem't dayly to take hold of me. And I have often thought I could have been willing to have gone this nation round like a poor pilgrim in want and poverty, so that I could but have witnessed peace with the Lord. And sometimes I have thought I could willingly have been rackt in pieces or buried alive, if I might have been freed of sorrow, and my soul saved. Many a time, in a fine spring when the earth has been comely to look upon, and the birds singing melodiously on every side, then have I gone mourning on my way, lamenting my condition and getting into hidden places to pour out my prayer unto my God. And when others went as I had done formerly, to pass their time in merriment and gameing, in drinking, in quarrelling, and idleness, then have I been exercised in mourning and prayer. When I have taken a view of the animal creatures, I mean the beasts and fouls that are here below, I have thought their condition to be good; for death to them would be an end of sorrow, but O! the creature man, if he died out of favor of the Almighty, he was of all creatures most miserable, because the soul after the death of his body was to live to all eternity. Yea, when things here below has been all pleasant and quiet, and settled in their places, the birds in the air, and the beasts on the fields and the trees growing in the woods most curiously; when the winds and the storms have been removed and gone and a summer season com't, then has my soul been like the troubled sea, and my condition like the waves of the ocean in a stormy day – one rising and swelling up after another. And O! I was so brought down at times, that there was nothing I could set my eyes upon that would bring any comfort to me; for if I had vast quantities of gold or silver, or of the most valuable things upon earth, I could have been willing to give it all, so that I might have had peace with the Lord, and that my strength might have been so renued, that I might have served and worshiped him that's worship and adoration worthy for ever. How that he or she that reads these lines, may not be case down, as I was at times, for I would need be thinking my condition worse than any man's yet though I had such exercises as I have here writ, yet, through mercy, I had a secret hop, that I should be preserved by the power of the Lord, for though there came such showers of sorrow upon me, yet my cries and breathings was still that I might abhor an[d] detest every vain thought and imagination, and, whatever came to me while here in this body, and I might not offend God, nor do any unjust action to any of the sons of men, but that I might live a life of righteousness in my day and time. Yet I was in and under these judgments, brought into such a condition that I had a real love to the sons and daughters of men, and hope I shall still enjoy or retain the same mind, for when I have heard of evil deeds and actions done by any of the sons of men, let their proffession be what it would, I was very sorry for them, for O! it was well doing that I travited [*sic*] for both in myself and others, and after mourning time. I did at times meet with brokenness of heart, and has been a witness of showers of love to have been showered down upon me, and a hope raised in my soul that I may be so asisted [*sic*] that I may continue faithfull to the winding up of all and the time that my natural eyes must be closed, this what I tenderly breath for, but some may think it strange I went through so many difficult passages. I shall answer what I believe was a cause, to wit disobedience to the call and invitation of the blessed truth in my bosom, and its my desire, if these lines in time come to be read by any of the sons or daughters of men, and especially by those that's young in years, that when they are sensible of the moveings of the spirit of truth in their bosom, against their vanities or evil deeds, that they join with it against those enormities and evil practices that the children of man are too much subjected to, for I believe if I had faithfully given up my well beloved lusts, I had never met with half the exercise that I did meet with, and I am further perswaided if I had not met with exercise in order to bring me out of these things which were contrary to truth, I could not have loved and pittied the sons of men to that degree that I have done and does, and desires to do, for tho' I cannot nor ought not to love a man's bad actions, yet I ought to love and pity the man so far as I yet see. I may draw to a conclusion of this piece of work – desiring it may not be torn or consumed, but read in fear by those into whose hands it may fall into, and it is the sincere travail of my soul that I may be preserved in hope, fidelity, and in true fear, and in an holy awe while here I may have a day, and the same I wish for other mortal men.

Timothy Cragg.

Transcribed from the original M.S.. by me, David Cragg, the 13th to the 17th of the 2nd month, in the year 1797. I writ at the rate of only four of these pages per hour. Tho' the original was good to read.

Eratums in this Book

1st. Page 3, line 15, for, 'came upon at that time', read 'at that time came upon me'.

2nd. Page 3, line 22, for, 'in the whole rigement that I heard of', read 'I heard of in the whole regiment'.

3rd. Page 4, line 7, for 'out' read 'of'.

4th. Page 4, line 31, for 'time' read 'year'.

5th. Page 5, line 1, for 'there and then', read 'then and there'.

6th. Page 7, line 12 and 13, for 'into whose hands it may fall into', read 'whose hands it falls into'.

These are the principle [*sic*] errors that I have made in transcribing the afore written pages.

I transcribed this for my own use, and the benefit of succeeding generations, that therefore we all might reap some advantige from the experience of a worthy ancestor and at this time, I being nearly 28 years of age, have undergone some very heavy and weighty exercises in order that I might be brought out of sin and wickedness, in which I was alas too deeply involved, and when my understanding was op'ned, so that when I saw my miserable situation, I was struck with wonder and amazement to see what a most deplorable state I was in. I cryed to the Lord for help, to rescue me out of this wickedness and sin, but for a time I had scarce any hope that the Lord would ever hear my prayers, and yet I thought if I be condemned to everlasting misery and entirely cast out by the Lord, I could not justly murmur, for I believed it was what I deserved, and if so I could not but acknowledge the justice of my condemnation, therefore I had nothing to trust to but the mercy and justice of our blessed Lord, who did show me the errors of my way. He also at times enlivened my heart with a reverend hope that I should at last be reconciled to him if I was obedient to the manifestations of his light in my heart. But how often I cryed O Lord thy will be done, yet never set about to do it, but did my own will, which is too often the case with us mortals, and at this time, tho' I have gone through a great many trials and exercises, and at times have been brought very low, yet I had a stubborn mind and will to be broken, which I must confess, tho' it be to my shame, is not yet thoroughly subdued, but there are many things that I was addicted to in former times, which I have been made to see was evil, and have been graceiously enabled in and through the Lord to overcome them. For a more particular [*sic*] account of my convincement read the 7th, 8th and 9th books of the history of myself written by myself. But perhaps those that see this may never see the said history. I shall enumerate some of the most matierial exercises and crosses which I was made willing to undergo tho' I might become the song of the drunkard and a bye-word amongst men, and accounted as a fool for Christ down and being made sencible of my miserable situation from which I was fully perswaided that none could release me but the Lord, and had scarce any hopes that he would ever hear the prayers of such a vile creature, yet the Lord took compassion on me for it was he that made me sencible of my errors. The first outward cross was in having my clothes made without any superfluetys, which was a heavy cross to my natural self and a reformation in speech, which was a thing I had taken great liberty in, also covetousness and reading vain books, newspapers and many other things.

An extract from an old paper written in 1723 by Timothy Cragg of the Chappelhouse in the forest of Wyersdale to the Trustees of Wm Cawthorne's will: 'First of all you may know by this that I have seen a writeing which plainly shewed that a considerable part of my tenement was inclosed of the moor as fell in my grandfather's time, and so with great charges, made serviceable for a family to live on, it being before ling and bent and pits and holes, as it appears in some places to this day.'

Henry Cragg, the person here alluded to, died in the year 1667, and his father John Cragg died in the year 1623, so from this it appears that the land inclosed between the year 1623 and 1667, a space of 44 years. From this I may conclude that this enclosure has taken place in the reign of Charles the 1st or maybe in Oliver Cromwells time. Carpenters had 6d per day in the year 1716 as appears by accounts, of work wrought at the chappelhouse.

Cragg family memorandum book, 1698–1816[2]

1698

February: – On the 11th a great fire in Lancaster which burned down about 20 Houses.

1701

October: – Great Storm: On the 3rd and 4th days at night the greatest wind blew that had been known for a long time. A great quantity of thatch blown off, some barns blown down and great quantities of trees blown down, some by the roots and others broken. On the night of the 3rd the sea broke into the land and some ships were driven ashore. The low parts of the country were overflowed. It was the second day of the spring flood holes. On the 7th there was the greatest flood in the Wyre known for a long time and most of the Footbridges were washed down.

1703

September: – A great flood on the 20th took much corn down the river Lune.
November: – It was reported that on the 26th and 27th of this month much damage was done by Wind at London, Bristol, Plymouth, Yarmouth and also at sea.

1706

June: – A Great Flood: – On the 18th there was the greatest flood in the becks on the North side of the Wyre that hath been known in our time. The most of the bridges were washed down, such as Hathornthwaite Haves, Leigh Bridge and Durnshaw Bridge. A great quantity of fences were washed down and much corn and grass flooded.

1708

April: – French Invasion: – It was said that on the morning of the 9th the French set sail from Dunkirk on behalf of the Prince of Wales with an intention to land in the north of Great Britain and it was afterwards reported that on the 15th 16th

2 LCRO, DDX 760/1, 'Cragg of Ortner Memorandum Book.'

and 17th the British Fleet fought them. They were reported to have 40 men of war and Privateers and 200 Transport ships, but the news being uncertain about the fight we know not what to believe. However it was said that the[y] returned to France.

December: – Murder: On the 14th inst. Thomas Mashiter of Marshaw murdered a man that was an old man and a pothor [*sic*] a man whose name was Christopher Erwin and buried him in his stable and paved it over and he put him in the hole on his head. On the 17th I heard that the old man was wanting and I was so concerned in mind and went to John Hathorn of Calshaw to consult with him and upon consideration we sent a messenger to Marshaw to enquire into the matter and the messenger having some suspicious talk we (to wit) John Hathornthwaite, Robert Bond, Joshua Hodgson and I went to Marshaw about day going and having two constables with us (to wit) Joshua Hodgson and Edward Winder of Hathornthwaite. We raised the neighbours as we went and when we came there the[y] said Thomas Mashiter was gone, but the neighbours told us that the said Mashiter had been paving in the stable some days ago and we searched under the pavement and found the body of the old man put into an hole with the head downwards and we pulled him out. We sent men from Darnbrook into Bolland and he was taken at Newton (to wit) the said Mashiter and was carried before Justice Parker of Browsholme, who sent him to Lancaster Castle, and when the said Mashiter was taken he had the old man's goods with him. He was taken the same night.

1714

August: – It is said that on the 1st Queen Anne died and presently after Duke George of Brunswick in Germany was proclaimed King of England.

1715

January: – Note: In these days from January 1st to March 25th was reckoned in neither or both years thus 1714:15 the Style was altered in 1752 and every month began 11 days earlier afterwards, as the 1st of January was formerly the 22nd of December.

February: – Great Storm: On the first day between the hours of 11 and 2 in the day-time there rose a West South West a most dreadful wind, which was over a great part of Lancashire and some part of Yorkshire if not further which did an abundance of harm in thatch, slate and overturning houses. It was so terrible that some people left their houses and put the fires out for fear of them falling on their heads.

July: – About this time there was a great uneasiness in the nation and many Presbyterian Meeting houses pulled down in several parts of the nation. It was reported that several were killed about it. It was said that at Oxford some mischief was done to one of our Meeting Houses and there was a tale of the Prince of Wales coming.

October: – At this time there was it is said men in arms in Scotland for King James's son, headed by one Earl of Mar and that they had taken Aberdeen.

November: – On the 4th there came into Lancaster an Army of Highlanders and Northumberland gentry and others. They proclaimed James King of England and an abundance of Gentry and others of the Church of Rome flocked to them and so they went on to Preston and took many men's horses. And at Preston the 12th of this month they fought as also on the 13th and 14th days with some troops of King George's and the troopers overcame them and took as some said above 2000 prisoners but when they came to Lancaster they were thought to be but 1600. There were thought slain on both sides above 100. The gentry they took to go to London with them and some of them to Lancaster and it was said to York and Chester. They then plundered several Papists' houses and then there was some little quietness.

It was said that the Duke of Argyle and the Earl of Mar fought on the 12th and 13th of this month and Argyle got the day. This battle was fought in Scotland.[3] When the army came to Lancaster the Country was sore frightened and hid an abundance of their best goods. The above said battle at Preston was fought in the Town and them of the Papist party would not come out. There was one Foster made their general and there was a man whose style was Darrenwater,[4] both of Northumberland and Dalton of Thurnham and many others. The said Foster was said to be a Protestant. They took an abundance of Prisoners and was afterwards reported that there was above 120 slain on the King's party.

December: – It is said that in the beginning of this month he that was called James (King James's son) was in Scotland, but things not going well on his side he went back again, but whither not known.

1716

January: – It is said that James at this time was in Scotland with Mar and they were providing to fight him. There was at this time an Assize at Liverpool to try those who were taken at the Preston fight and the Lords who went to London were called before the Parliament that was then sitting.

On the 28th there was 5 men put away at Preston for rising in arms, some of whom I knew.

---

3 Battle of Sheriffmuir.
4 Earl of Derwentwater. Sir Henry Hoghton of Hoghton Tower, near Walton-le-Dale, led the resistance against him in Lancashire.

February: – 9th of February, the Assizes at Liverpool broke up. It was said there was above 60 men condemned to die and several were executed at Preston, Wigan and Manchester. The news said that about James and Mar fled from Argyle and would not stand fight. They took shipping and got into France. There was some men executed at Lancaster and there was some hundreds of prisoners in Lancaster Castle who submitted to the King's mercy.

It was in this month that James went back from Scotland to France and Mar's army was scattered and that some of the Lords taken at Preston were put to death in London. Of them that was put to death in this country there was at each town a head set up.

May: – About this time they were trying the gentlemen that rose in arms in London. Several were condemned to die.

September: – In this month there was an Assize at Preston to try those who rose in arms the last year and some of them were put to death at Lancaster.

1717

March: – At this time there was a great talk of a plot that was discovered for bringing in some swords to assist James.

December:- On the 31st in the afternoon Christopher Parkinson who was born at Over Leigh went over at Wardstone to go to Harper Beck and had a daughter with him but she died before she reached the far end. There had been much snow and hard frost on the 30th.

1719

April: – This spring there was much talk of the Spaniards invading this Land and in the latter end of this month it was said there was some persons landed in the northwest of Scotland who were against this Government.

[No entries between April 1719 and 1781]

1781

January: – On the 6th news came of the great Hurricane in the West Indies at Barbadoes. Not one house standing.

On the 14th news came of the French landing at Jersey and all killed or taken prisoners.

February: 2nd the day appointed for the trial of Lord George Gordon.
4th: – Joseph Parkinson stopped payment. His household goods sold on the 14th.

March 17th: – News came of Adm Rodney taking Estalia Saba and St Martin belonging to the Dutch and 150 ships in Harbour and a fleet of 30 Merchant ships and 64 all taken valued at £2,000,000.

31st:– News came of the taking of the Ad Rodney privateer of Lancaster.

April 8th: – Went to Lancaster for Firs. The Old Town Hall down the Buller market in the Spring Garden St.

17th: – the Cuckoo heard for the first time this year.

June 4th: – Lancaster people rode the Boundaries.[5]

11th: – The races. Two sweepstakes for aged horses. Mr Pall's horse got the plate.

12th: – Cliftons Horse Surrey. Shepsted's Mountain. Newsham's Jenny. Surrey got the Plate and Clifton the stakes.

July: – The General Meeting on the 15th. The first year it was altered. Many people there.

August 11th: – At night a Scot killed by lightning in Quernmore Park.

19th: – Lancaster General Meeting.

October 4th: John Eshtown. Sale of the whole Apple Tree.

November 10th: – News came of General Arnold burning near London.

December 26th: – John Sandwal sale of Scorton Hall.

1782

January 19th: – News came of the French taking St. Martins.

February 2nd: – Took Lawrence Herdman's Estate for £32 per year now in possession of James Myerscough.

April 20th: – Saturday. On this day, John David Hull was hanged at Lancaster for forgery.

[No entries between May 1782 and 1787]

1787

A List of books which were commenced reading July 26th:
Parthenuna, a Romance;
The Life of Frederick III King of Prussia, 1 little volume;
Atlas Minimus Illustratus, or a deal in a little. An account of all the world;
The Memoirs of General Fairfax;
The History of that Arch Pirate Tulagee Angria;[6]

---

5 Ritually marking out Corporation property and administrative boundaries.
6 *The Arabian Pirate; or Authentic History and Fighting Adventures of Tulagee Angria* (Newcastle, chapbook).

The Siege of Gibraltar by S Ansel;[7]
Memoirs of Charles Frederick the 3rd King of Prussia, a geographical description of his dominions by S. Johnson;[8]
Marshal Field Europe by A. Boyer;
Sir Charles Beaufort a novel, 2 vols;
The Dean of Coleraine, 3 vols;
The Roman History, vol 4;
Tatler, vol 1;
The French Convert;
Athens Ancient and Modern;
Smollett's continuation of the History of England, vol 3;
Economy of Human Life;
Ovid Metharmophosus, Bachelor of Salemanca;
Guardian 2 vols; The Life of William Edmondson, a Friend;
Peter Quarl; Life and Adventures, Joseph Andrews;[9]
Rd Davies, a Friend; John Richardson, a Friend.

July 25th: – The Factory weir burst by a great flood.

August 10th: – The greatest flood in the memory of man. Sparrowgill flowed over the Bridge. Damas Gill overflowed much land and washed a deal of hay away. The Wyre washed the Company's weir out and the factory weir fender mouth and 30 yds of earth and did a deal of damage besides.

October – On the 28th was a bigger flood than the one of August 10th. The Wyre was $1^1/_2$ foot higher perpendicular. It overflowed much land and did a great deal of damage. It washed the Lee Bridge down which is a Hundred Bridge and the Abystead Bridge, a footbridge, Slains Bridge was washed down and some of the Wing Wall at Dolphinholme Bridge and the Sheet Bridge was greatly damaged.

December 9th: – A flood in the Wyre wore a hole 6ft deep under the Factory Weir and stopped the spinning for 2 days.

1788

May: – On the 12th Lancaster people rode the Boundaries there was 43 horsemen and 3 or 4 score footmen. They had 3 colours and a drum, a fife, a bassoon, a hautboy and a French horn.

July 11th : – News came that Lawrence Herdman has lost his trial about the stable ake [*sic*] which after a trial of 8 hours was given against him. It was tried at the

7 Samuel Ancell, *A Circumstantial Journal of the Long and Tedious Blockade and Siege of Gibraltar* (Liverpool, printed by Charles Wosencroft, 1784).
8 Printed in London, 1786.
9 H. Fielding, *The Life and Adventures of Joseph Andrews*...(1742).

York Assizes. At these assizes a man was sentenced to be transported to Botany Bay for stealing a bushel of corn.

On the 19th there was a very great flood in the Langdin and Hodder in Bowland. One man lost three acres of hay save only 1 cock. He had offered to get it the day before but thought it was rather too soft and left it for another day, but it was all but 1 cock washed away.

On the 25th a man made his escape out of Lancaster Castle. He pretended to be ill and his irons were taken off. It was thought he had got over the walls by the aid of ropes and has not yet been found. He was put in the Castle for breaking into a shop in Lancaster and stealing therefrom some ribbons.

31st: – The man that escaped out of Lancaster Castle on the 25th was taken again at Kirkby Stephen and as they were bringing him to Lancaster Castle again, when they came to a wood at the side of the road the man wanted to do his business but instead of that he got through the hedge and into the wood and his guard alighted off their horses (there was but two at the most and some said only one) and ran after him through the wood and through the wood hey lads hey. He there ran to where the horses were and mounted the better and rode away – fare you well and thank you. He has sent the horse back again from Otley.

August 23rd: – Lawrence Herdman has sold his estate at Greenbank to Thomas Bateson for £1120 and has advertised his other two estates, one at Appletree and the other at Whorehead to be sold on September 20th .

November: – On the 5th there was a great Bonfire at Ortner and upwards of 40 people present. They had 3 muskets and shot very often and a drum, a fife, and 2 humbug horns and shouted and hollaed and fought with fiery sticks. Several people were burnt and hurt.

This year was remarkable for the driest and hottest weather ever known especially May and June. Towards the latter end of the year there was a great scarcity of water throughout the whole Kingdom.

In October the King of England became melancholy or insane or starkmad, however he was deprived of his reason and there are many doctors attending him but at the end of the year he was no better.[10]

A list giving the number of Bankrupts from the year 1740:

Year	Bankrupts	Year	Bankrupts	Year	Bankrupts
1740	240	1757	284	1774	231
1741	265	1758	334	1775	381
1742	247	1759	289	1776	430
1743	196	1760	231	1777	430
1744	187	1761	198	1778	565
1745	207	1762	236	1779	491
1746	167	1763	259	1780	450

10 See I. MacAlpine & R. Hunter, *George III and the Mad Business* (London, Allen Lane, 1969).

1747	208	1764	332	1781	435
1748	167	1765	254	1782	560
1749	190	1766	283	1783	542
1750	212	1767	352	1784	531
1751	183	1768	295	1785	507
1752	166	1769	333	1786	494
1753	250	1770	287	1787	507
1754	232	1771	118	1788	709
1755	220	1772	173		
1756	274	1773	189		

Lancaster in 1784 contained 1783 houses and 8000 and some odds inhabitants besides Boarders and Sailors.

Greenbank vaccary in 1788 contained 12 houses and 72 inhabitants.

In the latter end of the year my father took of Thomas Richmond all the land at Greenbank at the yearly rent of £17. The landlord to set 10/- worth of lime on each year and to build a barn the first year. Taking for 21 years, to enter on the 13th February 1789. To plough none before it be limed and not to plough more than three acres per year. The whole is about 24 acres of arable, meadow and pasture land. The name of the fields is as follows: Infall or meadow, Pit field, Mean, Little Field, Great Field, Barley brow, Brownfall or Wingbrow, Holme, Little Crownfall or Little Wing Brow, Horsefield or Coppy and Moss Field. After that Thomas Richmond sold the house and barn, gardens and croft to Thomas Bateson for £100 and now the rent is to be £15 and all to be as was before but a bigger Barn to be built.

1789

January: – The newspapers bring dreadful account of the severity of the frost and snow from all parts of Europe. Several old people say that they never remembered to have seen so rough a day as the 13th January. A rag gatherer was lost in the snow at Cockerham. Several others were lost but were found alive.

March: – On Sunday the 22nd there was a terrible fire at Garstang which burnt down 4 dwelling Houses besides Barns and Stables and 300 yards of Hay. A very good Horse worth £25 was so much burned that died soon after and a sow and pigs were burnt to death.

The King got well in the beginning of this month and there was great rejoicing throughout the nation.

The newspapers bring account of the great quantity of snow fallen about the 13th of March.

The assizes commenced at Lancaster on the 31st of March and on that day Lawyer Postlethwaite dropped dead in the Court. The assizes ended on April 9th. 21 prisoners were tried and several were found guilty and are to be transported to Botany Bay.

May: – There was snow to be seen on the Fells on the 4th of May, the last remains of the great drifts. Snow has lain on the Fells since December 26th 1788 a period of 130 days. On Monday the 4th of May at night the shop belonging to Edward Richardson at Caton was broken into, goods to the value of £80 or £100 stolen, particularly £15 worth of Ribbons, Check, Silk, muslin and waistcoat pieces. All the tea in the shop and every portable thing. The thieves had sawn a hole through the door. On the next day some people came through Wyresdale and into Bowland to search for the thieves and at the Sykes they called to get something to drink and to enquire after the rogues. There were several clothiers and a stocking seller with bags like as Scotchmen use and when they enquired of him he made a wonder of it and said among other things 'Aye, all the rogues are not hanged yet' and some of the housefolk observed that he changed colour. However they that were searching went forward without suspecting him to Newton and Slaidburn and were coming back again when they met the clothiers. The Clothiers told them that they had a suspicion of the stocking man so the searchers came and brought the constable with them to the Sykes and he was there and had been all the while although they had been away four hours. The[y] searched his bags and instead of stockings they found fine velveret waistcoat pieces and muslin (but not a quarter of what was stolen out of the shop) and in the bottom of his bags they found two loaded pistols and two very sharp knives and saws, chisels, picklocks and everything belonging to house breaking. They then brought him to Lancaster Castle.

August 20th: – There is scarcely anything talked of at present but the lawsuit between Mr Hathornthwaite and Cawthorne[11] about Hunting and Coursing and Davis, Cawthorne's gamekeeper shooting Mr Hathornthwaite's dogs by Cawthorne's orders. The Judges came into Lancaster today. Their names are Wilson and Thompson.

On the 26th the trial between Mr Hathornthwaite and Mr Cawthorne came on. The part of the case tried was about Davis and Cawthorne shooting three of Mr Hathornthwaites dogs when he was hunting, but the dogs were not at full chase when they were shot. The trial came on at a quarter to five and ended at seven o'clock when Mr Hawthornthwaite got the Trial and £20 damages. It appeared in the trial that Mr Cawthorne nor anybody else has a right to shoot or destroy any person's dog whatever. Counsel for Cawthorne, Mr Chambers and Mr Topin. For Mr Hawthornthwaite, Mr Law, Mr Haywood, Mr Wood and Mr Cockin. The last mentioned is the best Pleader I ever heard. On the same day was tried a bloody villain named Kester Hartley, a young man about 20 years of age, for murdering his sweetheart, one Hannah Corbridge. He first gave her poison and then cut her throat in a most dreadful manner. After a trial of 8 or 10 hours he was found guilty and is to be hanged on the 28th of this month.

11 John Fenton Cawthorne (1753–1831), M.P. for Lincoln (1783–1796) and Lancaster (1806–7, 1812–18, 1820–31), lord of the manor of Wyresdale who resided at Wyreside Hall. He was impeached for fraud: see entry for 5 May 1796 and R.G. Thorne, *The House of Commons, 1780–1820* (London, Secker and Warburg for the History of Parliament Trust, 1986), p. 738.

The Assizes ended on the 27th. 12 prisoners were tried. 3 were condemned to be hanged, 1 brought in special, some to be transported and some acquitted.

On 30th October was such a storm at sea as has not been these many years and a great number of ships lost and men. The town of Shields lost in this storm no less than 400 seamen.

On December 28th the Clubmen walked at Lancaster. There are 11 clubs and above 1000 members.

[No entries for 1790]

1791

January: – 3rd Thomas Bamber took a large deal back from Ortner for the long bridge above Coormell[12] [*sic*] It was 53$^1/_2$ feet long and above a foot square. On the morning of the 10th Stephen Jackson of Galgate died very suddenly. He was in perfect health when he went to bed. About 10 o'clock he began to be ill and died at 5 o'clock. He was an eminent master shoemaker as any in this Country. He was a very cheerful good humoured man, but he has left behind him the worst natured wife that ever existed. He was buried at Cockerham on the 12th.

Almost the whole talk hereabouts is about the Horse tax which was laid on in 1784, but people not paying (only 3 in Wyresdale) the Commissioners have sent papers out to every person that keeps a horse or horses must pay or appeal. Most people in Wyresdale are for appealing and set off if they can. The appeal day is the 22nd of this month. The man who has done this good deed is James Hinde of Lancaster, an ill —. [*sic*] They are not only to pay for the time to come for also for last year [*sic*]. The tax is 10/- per annum and the Parliament have laid another shilling on so that they will be 11/- a year each horse.

On the 22nd, appeal day at Preston, all the farmers in the Hundred went to appeal, but only one Township got done which was Forton and most of them got off. When the rest of the Farmers saw they could not get to appeal soon they all gave 3 loud huzza's at which the justices were much frightened and sent a man down to see what was the matter and they said that they only wanted James Hinde, who was so frightened that he was almost at crying. The Justices and Commissioners then ordered all the Farmers to go home and they would send for them when they wanted them. The Justices [-][13] James Hinde severely for being so busy. The appeal day at Lancaster is put off until the 28th February and is to be on several days. Wyresdale is to be on March 5th.

On Thursday the 6th of January was the greatest and highest Tide ever remembered. It came a great height upon the Dykes in Cockerham and at Lancaster it

12 Cawlong?
13 Scolded? Original word is illegible.

run through the higher set of arches of the new Bridge. It is said the great arches were quite filled. It covered the Quay and washed many boats on but did no material damage, the people being aware of it, it having run very high the two tides before. At Pilling Lane end it had washed a fine new dyke down and a great many sheep were drowned. It is perhaps the greatest tide that has been since the 18th and 19th of December 1720 when it was down several houses and parts of houses and drowned 7 or 8 persons and about 20 Beasts & Horses & many sheep. Some people were forced to get on to the trees and staid there 2 days and 2 nights.

On Wednesday the 12th of January Stephen Townley was buried at Cockerham. When they brought the corpse out of the Church it was quite dark and most terrible wind & rain & those who were carrying fell & the coffin tumbled out of the Bier & would have been burst but as it was very firm, being good oak. They then carried it in cords to the grave which was very deep & when they had put the coffin into the grave 2 great Headstones which stood at each end of the grave fell in upon the coffin & they had never like to have got them out again. It blew the lanterns out as fast as they could light them.

February 12th: – There is a great famine of firing at this time all over the Country, but at the Morehead and Lancaster in particular. Turf they have none and coals they can get none at any price. The coal Flats from Wigan have been expected this Fortnight. They arrived on the 21st. Country coals were 2/- per load and when the fleet came they dropped to 1/-.

The Thames on the 1st February rose to an amazing height. At about half past one in the afternoon the water was fully 12 inches higher than it had been for 20 years past. New Palace Yard and Westminster Hall were actually overflowed and the lawyers were conveyed to and from the Courts in boats. This has happened several times before, viz in the year 1235, 1730, Feb 9th 1735, Decr 24th 1736, Oct 14th 1747 and Feb 9th 1762. The whole of Millbank Row, Vine Street, and Market Street were overflowed so that boats came into them. The Meadows and Fields from thence up to Ranelagh and Chelsea were laid under water. The waters rose through the shores and overflowed Privy Gardens, a great part of the Scotland Yard and some part of St. James Park – The cellars and Kitchens in that neighbourhood were nearly all filled with water. The damage done on both sides of the river in Warehouses & on the Wharves is immense. They were overflowed almost without exception.

On 28th February, the appeal day at Lancaster about the Horse Tax, and 5 Townships were there that day, which were Ashton, Arram, Bare and two others. They all came and several more. They had got some attorneys to plead for them which they did effectually, for the Commissioners or more particularly James Hinde had not gone according to law in any respect so they would be forced to drop it. In the meantime the Country people begun to be rather colypert and assembled to gather in great crowds and began to Huzza and shout 'No Hinde,' 'No Horse Tax,' and after a while they got a pair of colours (those that Warren and Dew had at the last Election) and carried them about Huzzaing, heaving up their hats and shouting 'No Hinde.' They went to the New Inn where the commissioners were and the Commissioners ordered the Landlord to go and shut the gates who told them he durst not, they then ordered another man to go and he did so. There being many people on both sides and when they were tired with shouting they wanted the gates opening which the man who had shut them refused to do. The people immediately seized them, got him down and hailed him about and almost tore all the clothes off him. They then burst open the gates and searched all over the House for Hinde but found him not for he was got out at a window and gone. The Commissioners were frightened and thought proper to let it drop and Justice Rigby came out, pulled off his hat and shouted with them and told them all was over and they might go home for they could not make them pay.

May: – 28th – A young horse belonging to George Edkin in Ellel had its tongue cut out by some person, in spite against its owner.

On the 29th a man was drowned in the Lune at Caton whilst bathing. His name was – [sic] Chambers and he was employed in the factory as a mule spinner. He leaves a wife and three small children and had he lived until the 1st day of June they would have had £8 out of the Caton Club[14] to bury him with.

June: – On Monday the 13th the Lancaster Club walking took place. They walked from Dalton Square to the Church 4 abreast and there was 1244 members in 11 clubs or societies.

July:- On Friday the 1st of July Janet Winder, a young woman and sister to Thomas Winder of Stonehead in Lower Wyresdale drowned herself in the Wyre near St Michaels below Garstang. It is said that she has been off her reason at times for some years & low spirited ever since the marriage of John Jackson of Lentworth, he having courted her at that very time. It is a pity she should have had a mind of such a worthless fellow as he is. She was buried on the 3rd.

On Saturday the 25th of June one Edmund Ryster of Scotforth got up in the morning & went into a barn & there he hanged himself. He had been in a desponding way a long time and afraid of being starved to death of wan although he was in moderate circumstances. A very illnatured man. The Coroners Verdict: Lunatic.

4th: – All the talk hereabouts is of the making a navigable Canal from Kendal to Preston to go by Lancaster which has been in agitation some time. They are for getting an Act of Parliament as soon as possible next session. It is 44 miles from Kendal to Preston and it is said the Canal will cost £1000 per mile only.

9th: – All the talk hereabouts is changed from making Canals to another affair of an oppressive nature to all who are not Freemen of Lancaster. There is one Mr Sharples of Lancaster, a Farrier and he has houses and land in the Town but is not a Freeman of the Town. The Corporation make those who are not Freemen pay what they call stalling money if they set up any trade &c. Now this stalling is no settled thing but the[y] make the people pay just what they think fit sometimes 4 or 5 shillings & sometimes more. Mr Sharples has paid for some years, but the 3 last years he has refused because he thought they imposed upon him.

14 Burial club or friendly society.

He only paid 5/- a year but they raised it to 10/- and this year to 15/- so he would not pay. They took him and put him in the Black Hole at the Town Hall – there he stayed some days and nights but now he is only a prisoner at large. There is one Bradshaw of Halton Hall will by tithes with the Corporation about it, [*sic*] he having persuaded Sharples to stand out so it is believed. The day after Sharples was taken he brought 15 horses to Sharples's office and he was in prison and could not be seen. Many other people came and wanted him but he could do nothing. There will be one or two Assize trials about it.

Extracts from a letter from Birmingham July 15th 1791. On Monday last in consequence of an advertisement for a Public dinner in commemoration of the French Revolution, at the Hotel in this Town, on the 14th ins a number of riotous people assembled and broke all the windows at the Hotel, pulled down and burnt both Presbyterian Meeting Houses, also Dr Priestley's house, Furniture, Library and Philosophical apparatus. The mob continued for three or four days and did an infinite deal of damage in Birmingham and adjacent places. The damage is reckoned at £400,000. They have destroyed 3 Meeting Houses and 9 other houses all belonging to the Dissenters. One Mr Ryland's house was burnt to the ground. A deal of the mob got into the cellars and drunk there until the house fell upon them and killed 20 of them. Some killed and some burnt to death. The mob did not give over until the Military arrived when quiet was soon restored. The inhabitants were greatly frightened and all business was stopped. They are now taking the Rioters up and sending them to Warwick Assizes for trial.[15]

The anniversary of the French Revolution was held at the Crown and Anchor Tavern in London where above 1000 Gentlemen attended. The utmost harmony and good humour prevailed.

Measure & particulars of a large Oak tree fallen the last month in the park of Sir John Rushow Bart at Rorthwick near Blockley, Worcestershire, judged to be about 300 years old which is perfectly sound & very fine timber.

Girth at 5ft from the ground 21 feet
Smallest Girth 18 feet
Length of Branches 30 feet
Solid contents of the body 634 feet
Estimated Timber in the arms 200 feet

	£	s	d
Supposed to be worth 834 feet @ 2/- per feet	83	8	0
Firewood	6	6	0
Bark	5	5	0
	£94	19	0

15 See D. Wykes, ' "A Finished Monster of the True Birmingham breed": Birmingham, Unitarians and the 1791 Priestley Riots', in A.P.F. Sell, ed., *Protestant Nonconformists and the West Midlands of England* (Keele, Keele University Press, 1996).

July 23rd: – Dr Sharples farrier is bailed although Lancaster would take no bail. They were offered £2000 for bail which they would not take. So he would go to York to the Judge there & as they could not hinder him he went with his guard & some friends and there the Judges took bail, himself in £40 and 2 others £20 each so he came back and at liberty till the assizes. The Lancaster Corporation is much mortified at his bailing. They hoped when he went that he might be put in Prison at York.

This summer there were 4 new houses built at Catshaw Factory.

July 28th: – at Lancaster there has not been so great a flood these 20 years (but one), it filled the streets from side to side. At Kellel there was scarcely any rain and at Cockerham none at all. Note: The other great flood at Lancaster that was greater than this is about 6 years since. It then filled the streets from side to side and about 21 one well [*sic*] it got in at House doors & windows & washed pans off fires & did much damage, washed pavements & roads up etc.

September – The Assizes commenced at Lancaster on the 5th one Davis was sentenced to be hanged for stealing a horse. He came from Manchester and stole the horse in Cheshire. 3 other persons were condemned to death, some were to be transported and some were acquitted. One of the condemned prisoners found means to hang himself and was nearly dead when found, but after every known means had been tried he recovered. When he was coming to himself he made such an uncommon hideous noise that all the people were frightened almost out of their wits. He was heard quite outside the Castle. On the same day another of the condemned men hung himself up but was found before he was far gone. They are now chained in such a manner that they cannot hang themselves again.

October: – On Saturday the 1st there were 2 men hanged viz Robert Davies for horse stealing and another for house breaking. They were very hardened and seemed to have no sense of their deplorable situation. There should have been another hanged but he cheated them, for in the morning when they had knocked his irons off, they left him to his devotions to himself and he tore a blanket into strips & plaited a rope & so hanged himself with it and was quite dead when found. The fourth that was condemned was reprieved.

On Sunday the 2nd Mr Grimshaw preached to a crowded congregation at Forton Chapel.

There has been a race against time in Ireland. One Wilde belled many wagers that he rode 127 miles in 9 hours and he performed it in 6 hours 21 minutes. He rode 10 horses and won about £1900.

On the 12th in the morning part of the Clough Bridge between Ortner & Cawlong fell down and now a cart dare not pass over it.

December 2nd – Today was buried at Wyresdale Chapel Betty Crosfield from Ortner where she had been 3 or 4 years. She was aged 88 years but had been in a decline a long time.

On the 23rd was buried at Cockerham Church James Brammel of the Great Crag in Ellel aged about 70 years. It was very bad travelling, the roads all ice and snow and very slippery.

1792

May 6th: – Sunday – I was at Forton Chapel today and my sister was thrown from her horse, but providentially received no great harm. Miss Brown riding on a Galloway and it setting off with great fury she lost her hat and wig in the presence of her lover William Holkinson.

About 6 o'clock at night Margaret Townley of Ortner died after about 3 weeks illness, being aged about 85 or 86 years. She retained her senses to the end.

June: – The Canal it is said will not get forward yet, although they have got an Act of Parliament for it, the proprietors thinking it will do so much damage to the land. Many shares are already sold out and it is said at £2 per cent [*sic*] loss.

Politics – In England the heads of Government seem to be much afraid of a revolution in England. The King has put out a long proclamation against seditious works and libels which are not to be read. They are forming a corps of soldiers to be ready against any disturbance and a deal such like as that.

The last papers bring an account of there having been a Riot in Maint Street London on account of the Magistrates taking up and put in the guard house about 50 persons who are going to meet at an ale house to make it merry it being the King's birthday. As soon as this was known the people came and assembled together to set them at liberty again. The magistrates would have dispersed the crowd but could not and then the military were called in and soon the crowd became ungovernable and began to break the windows of the Guard House and now the soldiers were come and the magistrates and constables in the guardhouse begun and fired at the mob – this instead of dispersing them made them only worse. They ran to the guardhouse and broke all the windows and would have got in there but could not. They then got the door off and entered amidst the fire of the enemy and immediately begun to pull all down and throw it into the street. The magistrates then let the prisoners out, all but 5 or 6 and then the mob became quiet. The next day they assembled again but did nothing but smash windows.

There was also at the same time a riot in Edinburgh on the same occasion and one man was killed and several wounded.

June 22nd: – The Proprietors of the Canal are taking a new survey and one for bringing it on a higher level. They were levelling today on Ellel Moor. They went a little below Henry Simpsons and across Wyre at Dolphinholme Factory.

July 3rd – I went down to the Pothouse to see a large ship launched called the Claredon of London, but it missed being properly launched. It set off and got into the water and run aground of the plank ends and broke the tiller and as it set off the male who threw a bottle of rum in its face by some means broke his thumb. The ship cannot be got off till next Springtide if it can then.

July 9th: – The great flood in the Wyre on Monday night the 9th was occasioned by a cloud bursting which burst in three places, on the Hinde Hill, another beside the slate quarry above the Townbrook and the third somewhere on the High Fells. Where the cloud burst it is said it has beat holes into the hard bent hill. At the

Townbrook it came down in a flood 6ft deep in a breast & came into homes and barns but I do not hear that it washed anything away except some potatoes out of a barn. All the grass was flooded, fences washed down and the road washed up and it is said to have done £40 worth of damage about the Townbrook. At Marshaw it was a terrible flood, the greatest ever known and came into the public houses there which is a long way from Wyre and at the gate into Marshaw Green the water was as high as the topmost bar but one. At Dolphinholme Factory it came down in a breast upwards of 4 feet deep. It is said that it brought down with it Tubs, Barrels, Butter Basins, Dishes, Stoves & other such like Things. At the street it was near as deep & came faster than a person could walk. It has done a great deal of damage in hay grass fences and roads.

July 18th: – our cousin John Clarkson was drowned as he was bathing at Heysham and another young man with him was also drowned. John Clarkson was apprentice to a stonemason in Lancaster and the other man was also a mason.

On Wednesday the 18th of July at Skerton during the thunderstorm the lightning struck a house and there was a man, a woman and 3 children sitting by the fire who were all knocked down and the crane and firegrate bars were melted off and one of the childrens clothes was burnt on one side to kinder and the child much worse. The house door was smashed to a thousand pieces & all the house much shaken as was two adjoining ones. At the same time two young men were passing the house with some potatoes in wiskets[16] on the[ir] heads and they were both knocked down and the wiskets blown to pieces. The men were no worse afterwards.

The newspapers give an account of a remarkable deal of dreadful thunder storms hail and rain in most parts of England and elsewhere and many great floods in some places.

August: – On the 15th the foundation of the intended new bridge between Ortner and Cawlong was laid by Robert Clarkson, Thomas Clarkson and John Green assisted by Robert Yates, labourer. Robert Clarkson having undertaken to build the bridge for the sum of £27 and is to have lime and sand found him and laid out at the place.

On the 18th the Judges came into Lancaster. There are 16 crown prisoners in the list for various crimes.

On the 22nd came on Cawthorne's trial with the proprietors of the Dolphinholme Factory about water courses.

On Sunday the 26th of August there was a most fearful Thunderstorm and a very great Flood. Sparrowgill rose very fast and it was as big as in any of the great floods in 1787. Damasgill was the greatest flood that ever I saw and it overflowed a great extent of land and did much damage, particularly to the groundwork of the Bridge and to corn and potatoes. Damasgill Bridge stands in a very precarious fashion. All the ground work is washed out and the bridge now stands only

16 Dialect term for basket.

on two stones, one at either side, that lower down the water is near washed out only holding by one corner. Conder was the greatest ever known in the memory of any person living. It has greatly damaged the Bridge at Galgate and made it quite impassable and the bridge at the New Mills is driven down. There are also 2 bridges at this side of Galgate near Smith Green of which one is washed down and the other greatly damaged. There are hundreds of acres of land under water in Holleth and thereaways. This flood in the Conder was bigger than Old Sim[ps]on flood which happened about 30 years since and was called Old Sim[ps]on's flood from this:-

One Thomas Simpson going to Lancaster it being Market day & he got as far as Galgate and Conder was remarkably big and out of bounds and ran over the bridge but Old Simpson would over and he was on horseback and he got on the Bridge and the Arch broke in & he and his horse slipped through the bridge & was washed down and landed in the field below and neither him nor the horse was drowned nor much hurt. It also washed the bridge at the New Mill down that flood. Old Simpson is alive at this time and lives at Hearsomesike in Ellel. Upwards of 20 people saw him sink through the Bridge and it has been called Old Simpson's flood ever since. All over Quernmore and Scotforth it was an unaccountable flood and about Caton and Lune was terrible it is said and many story's [*sic*] are told which I cannot well credit & so I do not mention them.

On August 28th Benjamin Clarkson was buried in Cockerham Churchyard.

On Thursday August 30th there was a most terrible strong East wind which has done an incredible amount of damage in this country both in corn thatch and trees. Accounts from Cockerham and other adjacent places say that the wind blew with unparalleled fury and had surely shaken corn, so ill that the like had not been seen for 20 years. It was done damage to the amount of £100 to Kirby of Cockerham Hall in corn.

September: – On September 12th was a very great flood in Sparrowgill, Damasgill and Wyre. It was a foot deeper than the great flood of August 25th. It has done a deal of damage in places and part of Cawmill wear is washed down, also the slopes Bridge at the Abbeystead and Richard Hathornthwaite's factory weir was washed out & corn overflowed in Lower Wyresdale.

October: – The Court of Wyresdale was holden on the 29th at Marshaw.

November: – On Tuesday night the 13th November the house of Andrew Richmond near Galgate called the Lone House was besieged by 3 house-breakers for 7 hours and at last they got in by bursting open the door by running the Cart wheels against it. They stole £40 in money besides a quantity of plate & got clear off with their booty. The[y] began to peep in at the window by 8 o'clock at night & it was 3 in the morning before they got in. There was only three persons in the house viz Old Andrew, Dolly Thompson, & a servant lass. After they had knocked the door down they were above half an hour before they dare venture in, old Andrew presenting a musket at them. At last they got in and wrested the gun from him after much struggling and that while Dolly got out of the house. The robbers demanded Andrews money and he gave them Two Guineas, but that would not do for them, they would have more or they would kill him, so he went upstairs and the robbers followed him and seized his whole stock of money, £40 & some plate of considerable value and then one of them wanted Old Dolly's money but the lass was not very ready to fetch it and the others having got so good a prize were for immediately going off, which they did, Old Dolly went & called Robert Taylor up and he went to Galgate to get help, but he and the brave people of Galgate were so timorous that they were above an hour before they ventured to the house and met Andrew who told them that the robbers were gone and he would not let them give pursuit.

On Monday the 3rd Decr the people of Wyresdale met at the Chapel to make a subscription to hire men for the militia and we subscribed 3/- each, there being 74 in Wyresdale fit for militia but they are not all entered into the Club.

On Wednesday 5th December was buried at Wyresdale Meeting House Jonathan Harrison, aged 60 years. He was one of the best men in these parts and formerly a speaker at Wyresdale Meeting and was very well approved of by all or most part of his hearers who were pretty numerous. Some four or five years ago the Quakers at Lancaster found out that he was not quite right in some point of religion, but what was not known and after talking with him they walked backwards and forwards and at last read him out of the Meeting and he must not preach any more. This was very distressing to him and grieved him sorely as it did all his hearers and it is believed he never came to the Meeting afterwards until the day of his death. He was attended to the grave by a great number of people and all his old hearers attended the funeral of this worthy man.

The newspapers give an account of the glorious successes of the French Army against the despot and slaves and Tyrants which they are fighting with. They have already all Savoy and set the people at Liberty and are still driving all before them. See ye tyrants the progress of Liberty and tremble at your merited fate.

In England there is some uneasiness and it is believed that Government is much frightened. Stocks fall very fast, 4 per cents last week were at 88 and about a fortnight before the[y] were at 100 and upwards. There has been several proclamations put out against Libels and Seditious Books said to be in circulation and I suppose The Rights of Man by Thomas Paine is one of the principal books against them.[17] That useless extravagant King or despot of ours has ordered the Parliament to meet on the 13th of this month, which was not to meet till January 3rd 1793, so that evidently shows fear to be amongst them; fear always accompanies guilt and also the King has ordered the Militia to be forthwith embodied in several Counties and two men of War and two Frigates put in commission so by that there is hopes of a Revolution in England, I for myself hope so as we have

---

17 On 6 December 1792, the radical Thomas Spence was arrested in London for selling copies of Thomas Paine's *Rights of Man*. The Royal Proclamation against Seditious Writings was issued on 21 May. See J. Mori, *Britain in the Age of the French Revolution, 1785–1820* (Harlow, Longman, 2000), p. 96.

been slaves long enough and have maintained the Hanoverian Despot long enough. They might find fitter objects to bestow £1,000,000 per annum on than a crazy King.

The English are fitting out ships and making a great bustle and in many towns the Gentlemen are forming associations against any alteration in England. At Lancaster they are doing the same. In Scotland there has been some disturbances in places. I rather think the English are going to fall out with France but if they do they will rue the day that they begun; but it will be the best way to make a Revolution at home. The pressing of men to man the ships with is a grievance and is downright Tyranny. The alteration which I would have is the total abolition of the Game Laws, for who has more right to them than the farmer who keeps them. Are not the hare, the partridge and the pheasant bred in his grounds, are they brought up in his fields and are they not fed in his corn, his wheat, Barley, and Oats. All farmers suffer material damage every year by this tyrannic Law. Secondly I would have Tithe knocked off. The tithe is a great detriment to the industrious farmer, every tenth sheaf is taken for tithe, every tenth acre is gone this way. Every religion I think should maintain their own parsons as they please if they will and not make every denomination of people pay to the maintenance of only one sort of Religion. Is it Justice! Is it right! Thirdly I would have that tyrannic mode of pressing men to serve on board the men of war set aside. Is it right to make a man fight whether he will or not? It is despotism and tyranny. Fourthly, I would have all tolls and such like abolished. One cannot take a load of meal or potatoes to Market but there is Market toll to pay for it standing in the market, and if we buy anything in the town there is passage toll to pay for bringing it out and if they be not Freemen of the Town. Is not this an Imposition! Does it not want annihilation and laying aside.

Decr 24th: – The newspapers of last week contain the meeting of the Parliament of Great Britain and the Kings speech and it seems he is going to declare war against the French for some reason or another. The Parliament debate hard about it but a great majority is for it, but against it is several good spokesmen and they let them know their sentiments pretty freely, particularly the Hon Charles Fox, Mr Grey, Whitbread the younger, Courtney and several others tell them any way is better than going to war, but fight they will, I suppose, and sadly they will be beaten. 'They will rue the day that they begun.' They can gain nothing but they may lose a deal. The French are trying the King for treason and very likely he will be beheaded ere long. I pity the poor King and think they should not put him to death. I would let him live but there is no chance of that scarcely at all.

Decr 30th: – This forenoon one Joshua Rigg, hatter, hanged himself at Cawbarn at Lentworth where he was found quite dead by Edmund Jackson & Thomas Winder. The coroners inquest sat on the 31st and brought in a verdict Lunatic. The account we hear of the affair is This – One Alice Winder of Abystead was coming to see her son Thomas & she came by Cawbarn & saw some body in the far end of the Shippon standing or hanging in a very odd posture and she durst not go in to see how or who it was, but came forward to Thomas Winders and there told what she had seen & so Tommy would go to see what was the matter as he thought it might be some of William Jacksons folk come to let the beasts out and was fallen ill or something of that sort. So he went as fast as he could and when he got to near Cawbarn he saw Edmund Jackson running up the cliff towards home as hard as he could. So Tommy went forward to the barn and looked into the Shippon at the West End of the barn and saw nothing there and then he went to the other Shippon and there he saw a man hanging but he was so frightened that he could not and durst not go in to the Shippon but ran back and got into the muck mudden and put up his hat he seeing somebody towards Lentworth who put up their hat again. Having considered a bit he ventured into the Shippon and took hold of the man's hand & found it quite cold & he found out it was Joshua Rigg. Presently Edmund Jackson had been there before, he just following Alice Winder and he found the Jos hanging up and was so frightened that he took away and ran home without knowing who it was and told their folk that there was a stranger hanged in Cawbarn. When he was taken down some went to let the family know what had happened and then William Procter went for the Coroner and he would not come because it was Sunday but he would come the next day which he did. Rigg had hanged himself with a cord which he had taken out of Thomas Procter's shop and he told the family that he was going to the Chapel & he would go by Ortner, but he did not go to either place, but to Cawbarn where he fixed the Cord to a bearer in the Scaffold bottom & then got a great stone to stand on while he got his neck into the noose & then slipped off the stone & hanged. His toes just touched the ground as he hung. He was taken home that night before the Coroner came. The jury were out of 3 Townships viz Higher Wyresdale, Lower Wyresdale, & Ellel. In Wyresdale was John Jackson, Thomas Bateson, John Townley & James Shaw. In Lower Wyresdale was Wm Martin. In Ellel Mr Fizzakerley, Wm Gifford, Rd Eccles, do. The Jury have 4d each allowed by the Town for such affairs as these. William Jackson's folk are so frightened about Jos Rigg hanging himself that they dare not come to Cawbarn in the daytime to let the beasts out unless two of them come together and one dare not go to bed unless another go with him & Esther dare not go up and down the house with a candle after it is dark. They have taken all the beasts out of Cawbarn home & will remove all the hay & corn as soon as they can for they dare come no more there. At the end of 1792 there was only one cotton weaver in Wyresdale, that is John Wender's son at Abystead, but there are several learning.

1793

January 16th: – There is going to be a great hullabulloo about Thomas Paine. Cawthorne will give something to drink on the top of Croft Height and make a great fire and burn the effigy of Thomas Paine and sing God save the King and Lillaballearo and burn heretics and when all the fools in the country met there are got drunk they very probably will go and pull somebody's house down for the good of the country and to shew their Loyalty to the King and Constitution. This disturbance is to be on Friday night next. They are making the effigy of Thomas Paine at Dolphinholme Factory. Lord help such fools.

Jan. 18: Friday. This morning a set of Tom Paine fools went with the effigy of him all through the country a begging to all the gentlemen's houses far and near but I suppose got not much. In the afternoon a great muckhide of Tom Paine fools assembled upon Croft Height and made a fire and then hanged and burned the effigy of Paine and drunk the ale but I did not hear that the King's health was drunk by any body. They shot a deal of powder away which had better have saved till the French came. Report says that there was 1400 or 1500 fools there but the greatest fool was Cawthorne. Many of the fools got drunk and then departed home without doing any mischief. It is to keep the people quiet and to keep them from making any disturbance and from talking treason! Is this a likely way to make people silent![18]

Jan 28th: – Monday – Cawthorne has got his trial with the Dolphinholme Factory Company. His cannon was fired yesternight by way of rejoicing.

The King of France was executed last Monday at noon so there is an end of him.[19]

Feb 2nd: – Saturday. John Jackson of Townsholme son of Timothy Jackson was married to my sister Margaret at Lancaster. The only company at the wedding was her brother Richard, Betty and Peggy Jackson of Townsholme and William Wakefield of Lancaster. The dues cost £1,16,9.

Feb 8th – Friday – Today Thomas Crosfield was buried at Wyresdale Chapel aged 89 or 90 years. Sometime since he was a farmer at Swanshead but lately lived at Ortner with Thomas Townley who married his daughter.

Feb 5th: – The French Ambassador at London has been ordered to quit England which he did. This is considered as a declaration of war.

Feb 7th: – When the French Ambassador reached Paris the most vigorous exertions were put into execution as War was unavoidable. They were determined to be ready to meet all Tyrants and laid an embargo on all the English ships in the Ports of France.

Feb 9th: – The French nation have sent another Ambassador over and he has been ordered back and the English have laid an embargo on all the French ships in the Ports of England.

Now sounds the dreadful Trumpet of War. There will be nothing but fire and sword, desecration and fighting up to the knees in blood. All Europe has taken the alarm and are determined to crush the poor French because they have thrown off the yoke of servitude. The English are determined with the rest of Europe to set up the same despotical Tyrannical form of government which the French nation has fortunately shaken off. They will strive I say to set up the same over the people of France again but I hope the French will be not only able to maintain all their liberty but to give all those who fight against them a most hearty drubbing. I must

18 The burning of effigies of Thomas Paine occurred across Britain in December 1792-January 1793. See N. Rogers, *Crowds, Culture, and Politics in Georgian Britain* (Oxford, Clarendon, 1998).
19 Louis XVI was executed on 21 January 1793.

say no more. My Father has commanded me to write nothing about the war or Thomas Paine or politics of any sort for if anybody saw what I have already written I should be tried for libel and perhaps hanged. If any disturbance should take place I should be first to burn this book which would grieve me ill.

Feb. 13th: – The Militia of Lancaster are embodied at Preston to be ready against the French, Liberty,[20] Land on the coasts of England.

Feb 23: – Great debates in Parliament about the war which has always been opposed by Charles Fox and others. On Fox's last motion there was a majority of 226 against it. For it there was only 44, though few in number they lack [*sic*] well and have much the best argument. It was a very great debate. Speakers for the motion, Chas Fox, Wm Sheridan, Mr Grey, Mr Adams, Mr Jekill, Major Markland, Mr Lambton, Mr Smith. Against the motion and for war were Mr Burke, Mr Jenkinson, Mr Bent, Mr Vaughan, Mr Porris, Richard Hill, Francis Barnet,[21] Geo Cornwall, Sir Hy Norton. Some members spoke twice viz Burke, Fox, and Sheridan.

March 9th: – Nothing material in Parliament. In the Irish Parliament the reform goes forward viz:- the Catholics are to have the same liberty of voting at election as Protestants have but the Catholics are not to be chosen Parliament men.[22] That clause was lost. The war with France will ruin all. All trade is at a stand.

March 9th: – The Judges came into Lancaster today. There are 14 prisoners to take their trial at the Assizes.

March 13th: – Was at Lancaster and heard the trial of Wm Holme for robbing Kester Lun on the Highway. Found guilty. Also the trial of a man for ravishing a woman. Found guilty. There was a very crowded court.

April: – The war with France is very ruinous to England and many severe effects have already taken place. Worsted is fallen in spinning 5d or 6d per lb. As one instance, one Betty Eccles a poor woman who spins usually 2lbs per week of the smallest sort which came to 1/8 per lb or thereabouts and a week or two since she took her week's work to James Jackson and it was fallen 5d per lb that is 10d out of her weekly earnings instead of receiving 3/4 or more she only got 2/6. She then was in a vehement passion and called James Jackson as ill as ever. She could (she being a rather silly sort of person) and thought it was his fault when it was worst for him of anybody. He said that although she called him so he could not be angry at her but really pitied her. I think those who began this war will have much to answer for. How can this poor old woman live now deprived of a fourth part of her bread? She must have more out of the parish to be sure and that answer is given by all the friends of war and bloodshed.

May: – The Parliament have been examining into the cause of the failure of the public credit of all the banks stopping payment. Fox plainly tells them that the war is the cause of all. The distress of the workers in the Factorys who are turned out is very great indeed. All is going fast to wreck and ruin. There are 160,000

20 That is, Cragg equates France with Liberty.
21 Burdett?
22 Irish Catholic Relief Act.

men women and children thrown out of work and consequently bread in Scotland. At Bolton people are nearly famished and money so scarce there that there is only one guinea in the town which is such a rarity that people give £ each to see it.

June 8th: – There is much mobbing and rioting in Ireland about the Militia being enrolled. Soldiers are forced to quell them and many men are killed in divers places.

August 11th: – Heard James Grimshaw preach at Garstang Methodist chapel from the text Luke 22 & last verse.
17th – There has been three sad accidents to horses lately. A few weeks since one James Procter, hatter at Morehead borrowed a horse to lead turf with of Joseph Smith of the Lee and he put the horse in the pasture and a cow sticked it with his horns so that it died soon afterwards. The horse was valued at 11 guineas. James Procter begged among his neighbours & got a pretty considerable sum of money to pay for the horse with. Peter Bramwell has had a young horse staked at an old gate at Damasgill side & found dead one morning last week. They were leading stones up the brow from the quarry and left one cart standing at the bottom whilst they traced the other up and on returning they found that from the stones being so much behind the cart had kicked up and hanged the horse.
August 22nd: – A very great flood much land covered. Abystead Bridge was washed down & all the last washed out of Caw Wear & otherwise much damaged. Dolphinholme Factory weir broken down in the middle 4 or 5 yds in length and the Factory water wheel gudgeon broken and another wheel broken and another great flood on October 3rd burst the Dolphinholme factory weir out. On the 26th it was again riven up and washed clear away. Not above one half of it left standing. The Factory is stopped when the weir is broken down. It took 8 days to repair it after the flood of October 3rd.

September: – A Mr Muir of Scotland has been tried for selling the Rights of Man and for sedition and found guilty and is to be transported for 14 years.

December 14th – The Parliament is prorogued until 21st January 1794. There has been many people tried for seditious libel and dealt severely with according to law. The weaving trade is worse than ever, many people almost famished and no sign of improvement. The war we are engaged in is the sole cause of all this stagnation of trade which has thrown thousands out of bread.

1794

On the 21st of January the Parliament met and the King's speech being made which was for bloodshed and ruin. An address was moved to be presented to the King which was carried by a great majority. The minority or those for peace were 62 which is 18 more than last year. There was [sic] great debates upon the address. The minority have the advantage in talking but the others outpoll them in numbers. Since then nothing material has passed in the Parliament House. The farce of Warren Hastings is to be carried on again in a few days.[23] There have been some debates in the House of Commons about the illegality of the Courts of Justice in Scotland or rather courts of injustice – they transport men for 14 years to Botany Bay for being honest men only.

Feb 15th: – In the Parliament House Mr Wilberforce made a motion for abolishing the trade of carrying slaves to foreign territories and after some debates in which J.F. Cawthorne and Dent had some share, the House divided, for the motion 63, against it 40.

Much damage has been done to shipping in the storm at the latter end of last month, a great number being lost, sunk, & run on shore in divers places. The storm and wind in the northern part was the most terrible ever known and many people have been lost in the snow in Scotland and also a great quantity of sheep.

March: – In this country many people propose going to settle in America – that Land of Liberty – as many as 80 are talked of within the space of a few miles. Two men viz George Parker of the Fell End and Samuel Roby set of last Monday (March 10th) to Liverpool to take shipping to America and look for a proper place to settle in to the happy shores of liberty and freedom and will leave this land of Slavery to those who have a mind to be slaves.

March 29th – My sister Margaret died today about 1 o'clock in the afternoon aged about 28 years & was buried on April 1st at the Back Lane Chapel in Lancaster. She had been married about one year.

April 18th – Sunday at Wyresdale Meeting was Sarah Harrison from America who preached and prayed to them.

August: – On the 1st there was new oats made at Cleveley Mill and on the 2nd there was two loads of meal of this years crop in Lancaster Market. It belonged to Wm Thompson of Cockerham.

11th: – There is a many shearers gone into Cockerham and over Lune to shear at this time, more than ever remembered before. Harvest is very forward this year.

September 25th: – George Parker and Samuel Raby are come back from America a few days since in good health and spirits.

October 3rd: – Samuel Raby and his father and the Parkers of the Fell End are preparing to go to the Land of Liberty. They have advertised their land to be sold on the 30th of this month. The Estate of Landshill is 160 acres one half belonging to Raby and the other to Parker. James Raby has also an estate called Starbank in Ellel of about 27 acres & some about the Hollings. Many more people talk of going. George Parker has said that in America a man may live as well upon £100 as upon £300 in this country.

---

23   Warren Hastings (1732–1818), former governor-general of Bengal, was impeached by Edmund Burke in 1787 for corruption and his conduct in India. His trial continued until 1795, when the Lords found him not guilty. P.J. Marshall, 'Warren Hastings,' *Oxford Dictionary of Biography Online*.

Note – lately Jackson Mason of Lancaster bought Gabriel Thompson's Estate at Greenbank for about £800, he kept it not a month and has now sold it to Thomas Bateson for £1050.

Note: On November 7th James Bibby's wife died at Catshaw and on the 8th Thomas Simpson at Marshaw. He lived many years at Hearson Syke, farmer and in many other places. He was an old man, but how old not know[n]. On the same day died Mary Corless at Abystead at an advanced age. She was walking out of doors on the day she died. And on the same day a child of Robert Townley's at Hathornthwaite.

Nov 14th – In Cockerham at the beginning of this week there died at one time 3 persons viz Joseph Poe and Wm Farrclough and a young woman. The two first were hardly ever sober.

On the night of November 21st the wind blew with terrific violence and did a great deal of damage all the country through to thatch and some trees were blown down and also Cawthornes slavery pole.

December: On the 2nd and 3rd there were very great floods in the Wyre, Sparrowgill and Damasgill. The Cocker and the Conder were surprisingly high, not only to overflowing the adjacent land but also came into homes at the Hole of Ellel and at Galgate.

On the 20th at night Robert Birkett of the Lee was as he was coming from Lancaster Market so benumbed with the cold that he laid himself down it is supposed and lay there upon the road on the High Crossmoor between 9 & 10 hours when he was found by his apprentices and with some others assistance he was carried to Thomas Escolnse's alive but unsensible where he continued till the 22nd and died about noon on that day. He never spoke nor was in the least sensible after he was found.

1795

January 12th. Timothy Birkett, hatter, failed and made a London fail. Supposed not to pay above 5/- in the pound.

February 4th. On this day 2 men were nearly lost coming from Lancaster viz Robert Clarkson & John Drinkall. Robert Clarkson was in company with his brother Thomas and they came by Galgate and at Henry Simpsons he was so starved and ill that he could not walk without assistance. They then called at his brother John's and got some refreshment and he recovered in some sort as to be able to get home that night.

John Drinkall, hatter, was found lying on the road by Christopher Gales who got him on to his horse & took him home and when he got off the horse he could scarcely walk.

Only the week before one Rushton of Tarnbrook or Durnisham Slater, was coming from Lancaster over the High Cross Moor road and had been near perishing in the Snow and certainly would had he not been in company with others who helped him forward & called at the Lee and got something to warm him so that he recovered and got home that night.

Feb 25 – Today was a fast and prayer day by order of His Majesty Tyrant George to pray for the success of his army against the liberty of France. N.B. It was a three halfpenny prayer but who composed it I do not know.

April 8th – About midnight my sisters daughter Janet Jackson died after a violent illness about a fortnight. She was buried on the 10th at Lancaster besides her Mother. Her father John Jackson is very poorly and it is supposed cannot live long.

April 12th: – On this day John Jackson died at night. It is very remarkable that in the space of about one year and a fortnight the whole family died.

May: – At the Fair at this time the Cattle stood in the Church Street, Pudding Lane and Penny Street, in the broadway pretty thick to the bottom and at the stone well and a considerable way on Leonard gate and up into Moor Lane.

On the 25th Lancaster people rode the boundaries. There was about 100 horsemen and but few on foot.

June 1st: – Upon Catshaw Fell there is old frost in the Moss which was frozen last winter. Where people get turf they find frost a foot thick and as hard as possible & when they have thrown it out it is 2 days in thawing. It is I understand thawn a foot deep and then there is another foot thick of frost. There has frost been found on the Abystead Fell this year.

The newspapers give account of very cold weather in Scotland. It had frozen and snowed for about 2 days and the roads were nearly impassable from the great quantity of snow. There were Icicles at the house sides 18 inches long.

July: – There is much talk at this time of the dearness of bread and a famine almost feared. A dearth it most certainly is. There has been 48 loads of Meal sold at Wyresdale this week at a higher price than was ever known before (prices from 42/- to 46/- per load). The greater part goes through the Trough of Bowland.

August: – On the 8th of this month there was a riot at Lancaster in consequence of the high price of meal. During the time of the market a number of raggelty women made a great noise and talked at a great rate and when the market was over and much of the meal had gone of it and a man called Taylor from Borwick had two loads which he did not sell. He offered it at 52/ lb at 50/- but no one bid him anything so he was going to take it away and had got a load upon his back and a mad woman seized hold of it and pulled it off his back and instantly there were 40 other mad women come to her assistance. The man seeing this ran away and left them in possession of the meal which they kept in the Town Hall above an hour and weigh or measure it in Littledoms but they could get nothing to weigh or measure it in. One woman swore she would measure it in her hat but presently came the Mayor Addison and others as Stanley, Turner, Cuthbert Baines etc, but they could effect nothing. The mob jostled and jowled them about so then brought some loads out of the Hall into the street and they gave many great Huzzas all the time. When they had got out into the street, they began to sell it out at 6lbs per shilling which is 40/- per load. What they would do with the money I cannot tell. Whilst some were with that in the street others of the Rioters kept possession of that in the Hall and the rioters insisted that there was meal enough and they would have it out. They would attack all the shops next and they declared that no more should be sold at above 40/- per load. One of the ringleaders was Rebecca Ashton of Wyersdale.

August 22nd: – There was the first new meal in Lancaster Market today – 2 loads belonging to R Whitehead of Forton and it sold for 42/- per load.

There was much talk about a strange thing that was to happen on the 26th viz that the Sun would not rise for 3 days and that the Devil would come and many people were so credulous as to believe it, but more especially the women.

September: – Dolphinholme factory which has been stopped since May 1794 as lately been sold to Hinde Hardman and others, who it is said mean to begin business immediately and Robert Clarkson has taken the Weir in the Wyre to build, the old one being all washed away. It is said that this company intends to spin cotton as well as worsted.[24]

About the 20th the Dolphinholme Factory people put a weir across the Wyre a piece below our Holme End. It is made of wood and by some said to cost £300. It is much higher up the river than the first wear and not so high above the bed of the river and a great deal stronger wood. They have to cut through the Woodridge a very great depth in a rock for the Mill race.

October: – On the 1st was Wyersdale Meeting. There were several strangers there – one each from Bolton le Moors, Warrington, Liverpool, Ulverston. One of them was called Burns and another Elijah Salthouse. There was also a woman. Several of them preached.

The 4th was Lancaster Quarterly meeting. There was many friends from most part of this country and three from America viz David Sands, Samuel Randall and Sarah Harrison.

At the Michaelmas Fair the[re] was the greatest quantity of Nuts ever seen. There was 220 loads of Nuts which sold at various prices from 4d & 5d per one-sixth of a windle & some at 10d per measure.

On the 29th at night the sea broke into the land at Thurnham, Cockerham & Pilling & overflowed all the land for a great breadth & did much damage in many places. It was the greatest flood or tide at Lancaster ever remembered.

At Robert Jackson at the Brows it overflowed most of his land & covered 11 acres of wheat & he had 2 stacks of corn which stood up to the easings in water. He had also 4 acres of Potatoes flooded. The damage he has sustained is reckoned at £200.

Hannah Preston of Hillam Lane in Cockerham had not a rood of land but what was overflowed.

At Rampa[25] the damage is estimated at £400 first & afterwards at £500.

---

24 See P.P. Hall, 'Dolphinholme, A History of the Dolphinholme Worsted Mill, 1784–1867,' *Transactions of the Fylde Historical Society*, 3 (1969).
25 Braides, near Cockerham?

At the Bankend much harm was done & gate stopps washed up that were set 5 feet deep in the ground and at Cocker Bridge it burst the flood gates.

At Isabelle Parkinson's much damage done and all her ground overflowed.

Two houses were washed down in Pilling and at Pilling Hall they were wakened by the Cattle bellowing and on getting up found them standing up to their belly's in the water in the shippons. They immediately turned them out and drove them on to a hill near but presently the water rose & covered the hill but not so deep but that the cattle could stand. In one house in Pilling an old woman was in bed sitting and the water rose about her breast high.

In one place above 20 empty hogsheads were taken up and great quantities of shipswood.

At Cockerham Hall much damage was done. Where the ground was flooded it is said that it is spoiled for 2 years & all the Dykes filled with salt water. There is no fresh water to be found on several farms.

At Lancaster much damage was done in the lower parts of the Town. Most of the cellars on the Quay were filled with Water and great quantities of sugar and other perishable articles destroyed. On the 29th the tide ran very high and a great number of people stood above about Lancaster Church to view it and saw it run up with amazing rapidity. It covered all Lancaster March & the Quay & floated a great quantity of wood up the Quay & at the New Bridge a great height & covered the Ladies Walk & spoiled all the ale in a Public House.

At Preston 2 sloops were driven upon the Marsh & 2 ships were lost at Wyre foot and 5 dead men cast up at Silverdale.

Over Lune much damage was done to the land and the dykes. A barn end was washed down in one Bagot's property a large hole was made by the flood capable of holding a large ship.

November 14th: – There is much talk at this time of the dearness of provisions, of a dearth of provisions, of a dearth and a famine, this years crop being reported to be quarter short of the usual produce in the corn countries.

November 17th: – Today the Constable and Overseer of the Township was about seeing what corn people had this year an account having to be given of the corn people had this and the last two years by order of the Justices of the Peace, Parliament having the dearness of Bread and Grain under consideration at this time.

December 2nd. On this day was buried at Wyresdale Meeting House Jane Harrison, widow of Jonathan Harrison, aged 68 years. It is 3 years less 3 days since Jonathan was buried.

1796

January 8th: – Dolphinholme Factory is not yet got to work but great preparations is making at this time. A weir has been erected over a Wyre a piece below our holm[sic] and made of wood like the old one but not so high by a deal and much stronger. In making it, first a half baulk was laid in the bottom of the river and was fastened down by spules 4 feet long driven through the bank. Into this was erected posts nearly perpendicular and on the top of these posts was fixed across a half baulk for the loss of the Weir and then it was planked on the foreside and nailed to the top and bottom baulks and behind was an apron or sail 6 yds broad from the Weir and from this apron was supporters set to the top of the Weir and then it was planked slant down from the top of the Weir to the apron and on the foreside of the Weir was laid Stones & gravel as high as the Weir and as broad as a cart road. A new fenderhead was made and a new cut or wull [*sic*] race made through part of the wood it turning from the fendermouth much into the brow side which being soft marshy stuff it slipped in almost as fast as they got it out. The men that made the cut had 3/- a day & potatoes, cabbage & onions & a house to live in. The Company have bought £4000 worth of wool and brought much of it to Dolphinholme and have at this time got 15 wool combers and more are wanted. The lowest account says they will have 30 combers and the highest says 120. They talk of employing about 200 people. At this time they have hired 3 blacksmiths viz Edmund Winder, James Parker & Christopher Beamon. Headwen is head generalissimo and John Patchell clerk at £50 per year. They are also going to build 3 or 4 houses in the Brorr side above the other houses at the other side of the road and have set the feighing[26] to Joseph Parkinson, John Swindlehurst and Pedder & John Halkinson at 2/- per day or 4d per yard and when they had worked a day or two they chose to do it by the day but since they would rather do it by the yard but must not choose again. The houses at the factory side of the Wyre are to be 1/6 per week and those at the bridge end the same price. The higher houses are to be 1/3 per week. The shop is nearly £10 taken by Jonathan Speakman. Anthony Phipick intends to Kit [*sic*] milk hither from Higher Greenbank.

Jan 11th : – The Court for Wyersdale was held this day at Marshaw and my father and Thomas Procter were appointed assessors and Thomas Bamber and John Hall were appointed Fence lookers and streetmasters and there is always twelve Jurymen chosen and this time three were chosen who refused to take an oath so they took their affirmation instead. Thomas Procter, William Cragg and my father. I never heard of anyone being appointed a juryman without taking an oath before.

12th: – Dolphinholme Factory it is said is to begin work next week. Hadwen is for finding the road through Wyresdale. He will have it made 8 yards wide. It is said he is gone to Lancaster today for that purpose.

J.F. Cawthorne is going to build a new Factory at Corless Mill to be 37 yards long 11 yds broad and 4 storeys high. To be up in 6 mths time to spin worsted. He has hired Nathaniel Booth who is to have the whole ordering about the factory. It is said they will have water enough and a fall of 20 feet. Factory houses to be built in a lot above the wood.

---

26 Cleaning or clearing out.

Jan 14th: – Hadwen of Dolphinholme has fined the road through the middle of Wyresdale. The road through Hayshaw he had intended to fine but George Drinkall supervisor of Wyresdale set some men to repair it & so he could not fine the road when it was under repair & so he for spite it is said fined the middle road which indeed is very bad in many places as the Cross Lanes, Longrake, Wyre and the Sheet Lane and from thence till it join the other road below the top of Emmets near the 4r mile stone. The road I suppose to be about 3 miles long or thereabouts.

16th: – It is now said that the road through Hayshaw that is indicated from Lower Wyresdale to the top of the Trough is not less than 5 miles long and it is reported that it must be made 3 yards wider all the way and that two new bridges must be made, one at the Mill Brook over Wyre and the other over the Camhousclough.[27] It is supposed to cost £300 or £400.

On the 16th of this month it being Market day at Lancaster and meal and wheat very dear though a good supply was there. In consequence of the high price of meal a great number of raggelty women assembled and threatened to take meal from folk. However the meal was soon over – in less than 15 minutes – the buyers only spoke twice for a bargain viz 'What price?' which was 42/- mostly. 'Tye it up' so all was over presently in the market. But Robert Bleasdale took a Cartfull down to the Bear and Staff and there a great company of women and some men collected about the cart and would needs have the loads out. But a country man told them if they would go to the Castle they might lay their hands on it, if not, they had better desist for everyone that made any attempt to unload the cart should certainly go there or to the House of Correction. Jacob Bibborough put three load on to the cart at the Bear and Staff, the man upon the cart was much frightened and thought they would have seized the meal but Jacob said 'Come, never fear, they dare not meddle.' So they got loaded and Robert drove off but was in such a hurry that he forgot his haystack. John Cartmell of the Marlholes came out of the Bear and Staff and got well called, the mob told him he had a rare broad back to whip. After the cart was gone the women accused one another of being faint-hearted in the affair. They then went to the Stone Well and back again to the Horse Shoe Burner as if looking for some other carts. They threatened that on the 18th they would pull Redmayne's Warehouse down. On the 18th accordingly as they had promised they found meal but did no damage. They then went down the Pudding Lane and insulted John Jackson, shopkeeper and then went to the Quay and broke some windows and then back to the Horse Shoe Corner and there was Wm Lambert's folk with a cart and a wagon loaded with meal which the mob threatened to take but the drivers drove into the Bear and Staff yard and the Landlord went and raised men and the Mayor and so they guarded the meal out of the town. The mob huzza'd three times when they got into Redmayne's Warehouse.

In the last session of Parliament an Act was passed for the more ready passage of grain from one part of the country to another and these mobs are not for

27 Damasclough?

letting it circulate but they would keep it all at Lancaster. In this winter there has passed through Lancaster many hundred loads of meal every week which gives great disturbance to Lancaster Mobs. There is Badgers, or traders in corn and meal going from Preston, Chipping and other parts and buying up all the meal they can from Kendal, Penrith and the North Country all of which passes through Lancaster and goes to Blackburn, Burnley, Bolton and other parts, but Lancaster is a place where the North Country people deliver their meal and carts from Ellel and other parts, take it forward to the South. Christopher Marton of Preston, a great trader comes once or twice to Lancaster for meal and takes 50 or 60 loads at a time.

In the north it certainly has been a good crop of oats but in the south that is Blackburn, Burnley and Bolton and other markets the crop of the adjacent country however good would not sufficiently supply them and formerly before they were supplied out of Yorkshire mostly, but since the war there has been very little corn imported at Hull and other ports and so the Yorkshire farmers find a better market the other way and nearer home.

Many people have got an idle silly notion that the wheat and meal is bought by traders and sent in to France to confirm what they say that a Person who had been a prisoner in France and going into a warehouse there saw many sacks with James Burnton set on them and others with Redmayne Lancaster and several other peoples sacks he saw. Many people are so credulous as to believe this story though nothing could be more silly and absurd.

January: – Note:- One Betty Procter wife of Thomas Procter died the latter end of last month and Thomas insisted that she should be buried in an old chest that stood in the house, however the neighbours interfered and persuaded him from it so he ordered a coffin to be made but told the Carpenter that he must never lay plane on the boards but just nail them together rough as they were. There were only few bid to the funeral and the corpse was brought in a Cart to the Chapel Yard.

On the 17th of this month Lyddie Barrow, Innkeeper [of] Garstang died & on the same day 2 children of Wm Kirby of Cockerham of a scarlet fever. On the 19th Thomas Gardner died at Galgate.

On the 22nd of this month at Lancaster a great concourse of the mobility[28] assembled.

Feby 18th: – Dolphinholme Factory: At this time they have got about 15 frames to work and spin very well. Some they spin to 18 hanks to the lb. They are going to build more houses, it is said, 12 or 14 in all. 6 men have been at work all this year in feying for homesteads in the Crow Side at 2/- per day till Candlemas. Robert Clarkson has taken the houses to build.

Feb 20th: – At Lancaster Market a man had some loads of meal adulterated with other grain as barley and peas. The meal was soft and doughty. When it was found out the man ran away and the Town's officers took the meal away to a place of safety. It is said there was 10 loads of this meal.

28 Military.

Feb 22ⁿᵈ: – Today was buried at Wyresdale Chapel John Winder of Dolphinholme. The farm is now out of lease, his life being the last. The rent was £44 per annum and now it is supposed it will be £100 or more. John had only one child at his death.

Feb 24ᵗʰ: – The Reelers at Dolphinholme Factory had a turn out last week and insisted on having the same wages as the last company gave which was granted. Robert Clarkson laid the foundation of part of the new houses this week.

There is to be a sale at Dolphinholme on the 8ᵗʰ and 9ᵗʰ of next month, Alice Winder leaving the place which she could not take again. It is vaguely reported that there has been £150 per year bid for the farm.

March:- On the 10ᵗʰ of this month one Sutton from Preston called at John Townley's at Ortner and being very full of himself he took a gun down in the parlour, pointed it at James Clarkson who was serving on the table but James took hold of the gun and turned it sideway and stooped down and so missed being shot for the gun went off against the hearthstone and the shots flew into the ash-hole & filled the whole room with ashes and smoke. Several persons narrowly escaped being hit. Sutton only laughed when all was done.

Last week a Hawk pursued a little bird into the house of Christopher Gates and the little bird gave a sudden turn, screamed, and flew out at the door again and the Hawk flew against the window and was taken there by Christopher Gates' wife.

About 5 o'clock on the morning of March 27ᵗʰ the barn and part of the house of Grifith at Scotforth was burnt down. The damage is estimated at £100. Among other valuable articles destroyed was 9 fighting cocks which were to have fought tomorrow.

April 9ᵗʰ: – At this time there are 4 stationers shops in Lancaster but some time since there were 6.

April 14ᵗʰ: – A coat and waistcoat cost 8/- making in Lancaster. In the country a tailor has 1/- per day and meal, but at this time some have got to 1/3 per day and meal.

April 18ᵗʰ: – Richard and I set off this morning to go to Carlisle. We set off at 2 o'clock and got to Kendal by 10 o'clock in the morning then forward over Shap Fells to Shap and from thence to Penrith which is a pretty large town where we tarried all night and we were much fatigued with our journey of about 55 miles. It was 7 o'clock at night when we reached Penrith. The day was very warm and there was a great shower of rain upon Shap Fells, part of which we were in. On the 19ᵗʰ we went from Penrith to Carlisle over Penrith Fell. Cumberland Quarterly Meeting was held in the afternoon. On the 20ᵗʰ the Yearly Meeting was held and many friends were there from various parts of the country and from America. On the 21ˢᵗ a meeting for conference. We left Carlisle for Wigton. On the 22ⁿᵈ we came from Wigton, through Cockermouth to Whitehaven, 31 miles. On the 23ʳᵈ we came from Whitehaven through Egremont to Kendal, 50 miles and we were much fatigued at night. We came over Hardknot and Wryness [*sic*] and by Windandermere [*sic*] and Ambleside.[29] On the 24th we came from Kendal by Milnthorpe and Warton to Bolton.

May:- On the 2nd in the afternoon as Henry Killgram and James Ratlif were coming from Lancaster both of them were very drunk. They both got on to one horse and were riding along but it is said not very fast, but they both fell off between Lancaster and Scotforth against a fence wall and James Ratliff's head was so smashed that he died a few hours afterwards. The other man was much bruised but not supposed dangerous.

May 5th: – News came to day that John Fenton Cawthorne is expelled [from] the House of Commons. The house divided on the motion for expelling him and there appeared for the expulsion 108 against it 12. Majority 96.[30] So now this tyrant is divested of all his honours and places and reduced to nothing and worse than nothing. An infamous character. It is also said that he has assigned over his estate and effects to one Green an attorney at London for the benefit of the Creditors and that his land will be sold very soon.

In the latter end of April there set off out of Lower Wyersdale and parts adjacent a number of people going to Liverpool and from hence to New York in America where they mean to settle viz:
John Richardson, his wife and 6 children;
John Shaw and Robert Shaw;
John Robertson and 3 daughters;
James Lambert, his wife and 3 children;
George Parker and his wife.
Some account of them.
John Richmond of the Lane Head in Lower Wyersdale, husbandman. He had two farms underhand, one on an old lease very cheap & 3 lives in it, the other he had from year to year at a very reasonable rent. Upon the whole he had a very good living in this country which he could not be deprived of during his life, but he was a whimsical sort of man and he thought himself of going to America and so could not be easy until he went. His wife had a legacy of £187 left by a relation at Liverpool very lately. His eldest child was about 18 yrs old & the youngest about 1 year.

John Shaw, servant with John Richmond had a small tenement in Lower Wyersdale. He was a young man as was his brother Robert Shaw.

John Robinson of the Stakehouses, farmer, should have gone last year and sold all he had but when the time came his wife would not go but she would never live with him after so now he is gone without her.

James Lambert, weaver, at the Lonehead [sic] at a place called Sanderses. He has 3 small children.

---

29 Hardknott, Wrynose and Windermere.
30 See page 61, footnote 11.

George Parker, late of the Fell End in Lower Wyersdale, farmer. He had a very good estate of land at a place called Landskill which he sold last year. He is one that went into America about two years since to see what sort of a country it was. He has about £1000 fortune. It is said that they sailed in low spirits and were very sorrowful to leave Old England at the last of all though before they thought there was no living in it. John Richmond cried much at Liverpool before he went on shipboard though he was never known to cry before. James Lambert was almost distracted and John Richmond's wife though the most unwilling to go was in the best heart of any present. About a year since several people went to America out of this country viz George Aitken and 2 sons. He had an estate of land in Ellel and one John Berry who was born about Orton and was farmer beyond Burton in Kendal. He and his wife and six children went; and one James Thompson from the Foxhouses, his wife and four children also.

May 11th:- There are now 3 arches built of the Canal Bridge which is building over Lune and the fourth begun of. There is to be 5 arches in all.

May 24th: – A General Election is at this time summonded for a new Parliament the other being dissolved by proclamation.

The Election at Lancaster took place on the 30th when Dent and Richard Penn came in without any opposition.[31] Penn is come in Lord Lonsdale's interest, Lonsdale having had 3 contests before at Lancaster and never got in. The fourth time he comes in without opposition. All the freemen's sons and apprentices had their freemen given by Dent and Penn. The apprentices cost £1.15.3 each and the freemen's sons £1.5.3 each. This is like making interest against the next election.

June 6th: – The election at Preston is carried on with great vigour on both sides. Horrocks is 338 votes. The Earl of Derby's two candidates 321 each and it is reported that Horrocks will gain the day he being supported by the Corporation. The Earl of Derby has considered the Borough almost as his own for nearly 30 years.

June 15th: – Preston election is over and Stanley and Houghton are returned. Horrocks has lost the day. The numbers were Stanley 772, Houghton 767, Horrocks 739. It is said that Horrocks polled all that he had and the others did not, having some which they did not poll.[32]

31 John Dent (1761–1826) was Tory MP for Lancaster, 1790–1812, and had a seat at Cockerham. Richard Penn (1734–1811) was Tory MP for Lancaster, 1796–1802, and was patronised by the Westmorland magnate Lord Lowther. Thorne, *House of Commons*, pp. 587, 758.
32 Sir Henry Houghton (1728–95) and his son Henry (1768–1835) represented the Whig interest at Preston from 1768 to 1802, in coalition with Lord Stanley (1775–1851), the Earl of Derby's relation, from 1796. The rapid rise of the Horrocks brothers John (1768–1804) and Samuel (1766–1842), who created the largest manufacturing firm in Preston, threatened the electoral dominance of the Earl of Derby, causing bitter party rivalries at the 1796 election. The Horrockses were Tories. John was elected for Preston in 1802, and was replaced at his death by his brother in 1804, who was MP until 1826. Thorne, *House of Commons*, pp. 213, 215, 248.

July 6th: – There was a town's meeting today at the Chapel about the moles and their catcher there being much talk about that affair and it is likely to be an endless cause of dispute and falling out about. Some being for doing one way & some another as best suits their own interests.

July 25th: – There was a sale at Galgate today of an Estate of about 20 acres belonging to William Procter at the Smith Green and it sold for £1314. William has had it about 12 years and he gave £817 for it and he bought the tithe afterwards for about £60 so he has gained in 12 years upwards of £400.

August: – It has been reported many times that at Dolphinholme Factory they spin very badly and make bad stuff and that they do not keep their wheels in order and the worst account says they lose £100 per week. They employ about 150 hands in all and some at a very good wage. There is 30 woolcombers and 4 assistants who earn £40 per week every week a blacksmith 25/- per week a clerk £50 per year. Engineer £2 2s per week and several others at a great price but the wages of the commonality is very low. One of the masters has said that if they had the wool for nothing their yarn would not pay the workmen's wages so by that it is doing very badly. They spin no more than 16 packs per week though the other company spin about 30 with the same hands. So by all accounts they are doing very badly and unless they mend very soon will be bred and liver up [*sic*] with loss.

August 24th: – A few days since two large seafish were caught – one near the thorn bank below Glasson Point and the other about the buoys. The name of them is not yet ascertained. In this country some people call them porpoises, some call them bottlefish, and other different names. One of them was brought to Lancaster and the other landed at the Thorn Bank. One of them is 21 feet 10 inches long & the other 24 feet 10 inches long and about 14 feet in circumference in the thickest place. There is much talk about them and many people have gone for the purpose of looking at them, but I hear no good description of them only about the taking & killing of them which is retailed out at great length but it seems so horrid and barbarous that I do not choose to retail it over here at any length save only that they were killed with pitchforks and Scythes and other mixed weapons. They made the water as red as blood for many yards. They are reported to be worth £40 each and are cutting up for oil.

The 24th of this month was the appeal day at Lancaster about the Horse Act and Dogs. I did not hear that any appealed about dogs or work horses but about saddle horses many appealed but few got off. The Commissioners made the appellants take an oath to answer any question that was asked them and then they asked if they never rode to see a friend and if they had they were to pay but some swore through all and got off. There is only one saddle horse paid for in Wyresdale at this time but it is expected that next year a great number will be brought into the list of Saddle Horses. The tax on such horses is 20/- a year and ten per cent on that tax. The tax on Workhorses is 2/- each per year. The tax on our dogs is 3/- each dog per year. If one person have 2 curs they are 5/- each dog etc.

There was a sale of land in Ellel at the latter end of the month belonging to General Pennington of Hampson. There were two estates, one at Hampson Green and the other upon Ellel Moor called Chipping Road tenement consisting of 44 acres of land statute measure & a good horse and barn which sold for £624 to Ed. Rigby Esq of the Grange. The estate at Hampson was 36 acres statute measure and was sold to one Fox in Cockerham for the sum of £1500.

September 16th : – Dolphinholme Factory. The company giving but little wages to the people employed in the Factory and the people discontented many of them have left the place being hired to another factory below Englewhite called Brooksbottom, some families getting 10/- a week more there than at Dolphinholme. The best family at Dolphinholme would have staid if they would have advanced them 1/6 a week which was not agreed to though at the same time they were in great want of hands. It is said that Hadwen who is chief actor at Dolphinholme is a very quick promiser but a very slow performer, and he will say anything and observe nothing as he ought to do. So many hands have left them that they were at the end of last week obliged to stop one third of the frames that had been at work since they begun and when they had the most at work they had not above half of the frames in the factory at work. The wages of the persons employed in the factory are not sufficient for their subsistence. It is said that their wages for three weeks will only keep them a fortnight. But the company propose to begin and keep a shop wherein they will fit the persons employed in the factory with necessaries at prime cost and stop their wages every three weeks so it is suggested that that shop will get all the people's wages and there will be nothing left for any other persons. They set up a shop not a year since to one Jonathan Speakman at near £10 per year and now they have given him notice to quit but as he was not willing they will set up another shop against him and ruin him if they can.

It is reported that the factory people are extremely lousy and dirty. One row of houses has taken or gotten the name of Lousy Row, a very scandalous name. On the other side Wyre all the better sort live and so it is by some called Quality Row and Quality Street by others.

Sept 11th: – James Sheppard of Lower Wyresdale who died last week was this day buried at Church town. A man of good circumstances in this world but of a fretful impatient disposition of mind.

Sept 20th: – Thos Townley's folk reared a building which they call a parlour and at night they had some drink and so became quarrelsome in their cups and got to fighting and Thos Winder and Wm Bibby got each a couple of black eyes.

Sept 21st: – A great flood in the Wyre today greatly damaged the Weir at Dolphinholme by pit falling the Apron or Sail of the Weir and blowing it up. It was supposed that the apron of the Weir was laid so low that it could never pitfall it or wash the gravel away below the Weir but that the apron would always be covered a considerable depth with water but some floods have proved the contrary for now the end of the river is worn some feet deeper below the weir than it was when the Weir was made.

Sep 24th: – At Dolphinholme factory all the folk in the Factory turned out in the morning for an increase of wages. They all went from the factory up Lodgholm and towards Cawthorne's. Steel and Hadwen, the masters did not know what steps to take but Steel went and got before them and would have stopped them or persuaded them to turn back but one of them run by him and the rest ran after like a flock of unlucky sheep. They shouted and huzza'd very hard. In the afternoon they came back and played at ball and the Factory stood still all day. They are in a very critical way at Dolphinholme they want hands very ill and those that they have are leaving them every day.

Sept 29th: – At Dolphinholme Factory all the workmen and others are come into the Factory again without any advance of wages. They say that they will try their masters for three weeks and trust to their generosity. When they turned out 50 or 60 of them went all in company to Lancaster to Captain Hinde to beg for more wages, but he had no hand with the Factory, it was his son and he was at Liverpool so they came back as they went. A rough ragged company like as of some poor house had been broken loose.

There has been upwards of 20 men repairing the weir this 2 or 3 days fixing the apron down again and stopping the leak by puddling. They have driven a row of piles just by the lower edge of the apron. Cawmill wear is also washed out so that there is only 2 whole paves left in the Weir. It was repaired only about 2 months since.

October 4th: – There was buried this day at Wyresdale Chapel Agnes Parker wife of Robert Parker of Greenbank aged 48, after an illness of 19 weeks. Her loss much lamented by her husband and children.

On the 21st of September two young men were drowned near Glasson, they being it is supposed drunk. They went from Pear Hall for the purpose of wading over Lune to Orton at which time it was a very great fresh flood and so rough that a boat could not venture over and it was dark at night and in making the attempt both were drowned. There was nobody present and none thought that they would have been so mad as to make the attempt as it was that time impassable either to wade or swim over or get over in a boat. They have both been found since.

October 5th: – Joshua Bibby of Marshaw came today gathering the Land tax and Window money and other assessed taxes, there being several new taxes that take place this year, as the tax on dogs which in Wyresdale raises the sum of £9 and the Horse Tax 2/- per work horse, there being 133 entered which raises the sum of £13,6s. There was only 1 saddle horse entered in Wyresdale.

On the 3rd Octr two Justices, Slainbank & Rigby came through Wyresdale to view the roads and to take measures with us accordingly, the roads not being fine enough for some newly sprung up gentlemen in this county (Hadwen of Dolphinholme).

Some time since John Drinkall of the Abystead vaccary let his farm to John Swindlehurst of the Little Cragg End in Ellel for the sum of £20 per year and now John Swindlehurst rues and declares he will not have it.

October 11th: – Last week died at Newton Samuel Harrison, a Friend, brother to Jonathan Harrison who died some years since.

October 12th: – A tremendous thunderstorm with hail and rain at Lancaster. The lightning was vivid and the thunder loud and near and the hail fell so fast that the like was scarcely ever seen. The hail stones were very large and came with such force that it was expected all the windows would be broken. The storm was of short duration but it made the channels run so as to be hardly passable. There was a very slender fair and not much to do amongst the clothiers.

There was a horsing race between the 3 mile stone and Burrow Bridge, it being a mile and a piece, between Kettlewell, Butcher of Lancaster and a man from Manchester for 50 guineas. The man from Manchester won the race by about 200 or 300 yards Kettlewell's horse though higher than the other yet had no chance for the other went so fast that it kept all the other horses on full gallop. There were about 100 horses and perhaps 1000 people present at the race. It is said that a deal of people are taken in, Kettlewell being thought sure to win the race.

At the Abystead there has been no bridge over the Wyre for some years, the old one having been washed away and broken so many times as at last to be quite unrepairable, but great complaints having been made the town at last agreed to make a new one. Thomas Procter being the supervisor this year, he and some others proposed to have a Spring Bridge which would they said be cheaper and stronger than a single Cale Baulk. They bought Wood and have made a bridge but have not yet laid it up and as some people say it will do no good and others say it is the best bridge that could be made of wood.

The New Parliament met sometime since and the Kings speech being read an address was voted without any contradiction, the King being desirous that peace should be established whenever the French Republic should agree to accept fair and moderate terms. Lord Malmsbury has gone over as ambassador to Paris to treat with the convention there and offer them such proposals as the English are willing to make but it is doubtful this Government will not offer such terms as the Republicans will acceed [*sic*] to.

In the meanwhile, this government spread the alarm of an Invasion which they say the French are intending to make and are making vast preparations for but I don't believe that the French intend any such thing serious. I believe it is all a scheme of this Government to raise both more men and more money and the Chancellor of the Exchequer has made a proposal to raise 102,000 men this year, viz 60,000 New Militia to be raised by the County as usual and 15,000 for the Army and Navy to be raised by the taxed houses and 20,000 horsemen to be raised out of those who pay for saddle horses, every tenth man being to go and then all the Gamekeepers in the Kingdom is to go they being calculated at 7000. All this vast force is to be trained and to be in readiness against the French make a descent on our coast.

Serjeant Adis has obtained leave to bring in a Bill for the relief of the Quakers in the case of Tithes putting it out of the Claimants power to imprison them while they have any property left and that also affirmation shall be taken in criminal cases, but this latter part I do not wish to get forward.

Oct. 26th: – Richard, Timothy and I viewed Dolphinholme Estate today and reckoned it to 98$^1/_2$ acres of arable pasture and meadow land besides about 15 acres of wood. We supposed the place would keep 28 gails [*sic*] and mow 18 plough 16 acres per year.

12 cows will make per year £60,
6 beasts to sell every year 48,
35 load of meal at 30/- per load 52
= £160.
Clearing poor taxes constables rolls land and other taxes tithe &c £20.
Servants and housekeeping bills £20.
Interest for £500 at 4% 12 = £52.
= £108.
Rent £100,
leaving for profit if the rent be no more than £100 a year £8.

On the 27th my father and Thomas went to Garstang to talk to Robert Mitchinson about taking the farm at Dolphinholme. He was very kindly but did not fix a rent of the place and so they did not take it.

October 25th: – Cawthorne's estate called the Coal was sold today to Justice Butler for the sum of £3440. It is let for about £80 per annum.

The Surveyors of Wyresdale on the 24th of this month went to view the road above Catshaw and found it in tolerable repair only one place they concluded must be widened forthwith and so people are warned in to go and work there on the 31st of this month. This is the only place that the Justices found fault with when they came to view the roads in the beginning of this month. The Abystead bridge gets none forward and so lies broken upon the bank of the river. They purpose to buy more wood for springers underneath. Some are for buying the best oak tree they can find and others are against it.

The Bridge was viewed on the 31st of this month by the Surveyors of the roads and they agreed to buy 2 five inch planks and 12 inches broad and 30 feet long for springers in the room of those that have broken and they proposed to have it laid up on the 8th of November.

The Parliament Sergeant Adiar [*sic*] has brought us a Bill for the relief of the Quakers which was read a first time. The Militia Bill also gets forward and all the other Bills for raising men are likely to go forward without much opposition.

November: – On the 1st part of Cawmill wear was washed out by a big flood.

Some time since the Corporation of Preston and some of the inhabitants entered into a combination to reduce the price of butter, which was at the enormous sum of one shilling per lb so they bound themselves on a penalty not to buy butter above 11d per lb but that scheme not having the desired effect and markets continuing as high as ever they therefore would by another method and they hired one Christopher Marten to buy butter over the Sands and bring it to Preston and sell it in the market to a certain class of people at 8^{1}/$_{2}$ per lb but in this they will lose considerably as butter cannot be bought at that price in any country.

Novr 17th: – The Abystead Bridge was laid up today, there having been no bridge there for upwards of a year. This Bridge is not yet finished it wanting the Pebbles putting on and fixing down and fastening so it may not tumble over.

The road is got widened above Catshaw and now perhaps it may suit little Hadwen and the Justices. Hadwen having indicted it some time since but the Justices pretended that they could pass it over if it was widened in that particular place above Catshaw so now we shall see how matters will go about this affair.

The Supplementary Militia Bill is passed and it takes all in from 15 to 55 years of age which will increase the lists very much. In Wyresdale there was but about some 68 in the old lists but this will almost double that number. Some say every tenth man must be polled, some say every seventh man and some suppose that men will cost £20 each.

Of those new Militia there is to be 5160 raised in Lancashire which is more than any county in England except in Middlesex and Yorkshire. It is said that this Bill creates much uneasiness in the country and the great towns and indeed well it may for it is a very heavy burden upon the people and who have probably a right to complain if they have a right to do anything else but why should a part of the people choose Governors and these Governors make laws for the whole nation – yea – govern them with a rod of iron and heap burden on an oppressed people already pressed down and groaning under former loads. I am for my part surprised that people of all denominations throughout this oppressed nation should lamely bear so many be many and such [sic] heavy burdens and so many oppressive laws and so many taxes, for now the long boasted freedom and liberty of Englishmen is all done away and not so much as a shadow of either remains. We are now nothing but abject slaves subject to the will and caprice of a despotical tyrannical Government. But I plainly see what the end will be if the people bear with it and they are so abject and abased that they will bear anything without offering to kick their masters or throw off their loads and if they will bear and continue blindly subject to the whim and caprice of their Governors they may and their [sic] or I may say our Governors will have all we are possessed of and then make us all Slaves and use us as the poor Africans are used in the West Indies; and this is my opinion that they will have all, and that is what they are aiming at.

In Ellel, they have lotted for a militia man, one of their old ones having deserted. The man that is lotted is to serve five years either by substitute or else serve himself. The whole township entered into a subscription to hire a substitute. There were 96 men in the list and they subscribed 3/- each.

In Ellel there is about 20 Hackney horses entered and one is to be lotted out of every ten to serve as cavalry which will call those that have one saddle horse entered £4 or £5 each, but in Wyresdale there is only 1 saddle horse entered though I suppose they will not escape so easily next year.

This year the Horse Tax of 2/- per horse took place and the Dog Tax of 3/- per dog and 5/- for dogs of other denominations and one Christopher Gates of the Summer House Head in this Dale refused to enter his dog and the Commissioners being informed those of Christopher was threatened to be fined and which frightened him so much that he went to Lancaster to get it entered but could not and he went three times to Lancaster and the third time he got it entered but it cost him 4/6 and thought he escaped very well. Thomas Kitchen of Lentworth Vaccary a very warm advocate for the war and this Government and stark mad loyal and hot against the French had two horses one of which was a young one and had not wrought much but so much that its shoulders were sore, so he entered but one, but it being much talked about in the country and John Drinkall a great newsmonger and a Republican talked of this horse to Francis Smith the assessor of the

Land Tax and Window money and other assessed taxes and John told Francis that unless he made Thomas Kitchen enter his other horse he would inform of Francis for neglecting his duty whereupon Thomas Kitchen went to Lancaster and got his horse entered. But Thomas was so vexed that he would inform of John Drinkall who had a dog some time the last year but had none when the account was taken of the dogs, so Thomas Kitchen threatened George Drinkall that if he did not force John Drinkall to enter his dog he would make a complaint against him so George was frightened and went to John Drinkall to talk about his dog and asked John what he might do and John told he might do as he thought proper but if he George Drinkall, would make a complaint against him for suffering William Cragg of the Abystead to escape entering his horses, he having four and entered but one and so all is dropped about these things at this time.

A load of meal at Lancaster 240 lbs at Preston 240 lbs
Do. wheat do. 280 lbs do. 220 lbs
Do. Potatoes do. 3 bushels do. 3½ bushels
A pound of butter at Lancaster 18 oz at Preston and Garstang 16 oz.

November 28th: – Today Francis Smith assessor for Wyresdale for the year 1795 came about taking an account of all the farmers in Wyresdale that farmed £40 per year or had an Estate worth £35 per annum a list of which he was to return to the Commissioners of Lonsdale Hundred at the weekend every one farming £40 a year or having £35 per year of their own land will be obliged to enter a saddle horse which will be 22s a year and at this time there is a bill passed for the raising of men to defend this kingdom against the Republic of France which threatens an invasion of this Country or at least our Governors pretend so, and therefore to be ready in case the French should put their threats into execution the Parliament have passed several bills for the raising of men and one of these Bills is for the raising of 20,000 irregular cavalry, to be lotted out of those that keep horses for the use of riding and they suppose every farmer that farms £40 per year keeps his saddlehorse, and therefore whether he keeps one for that purpose or not he is compelled to enter one as such, and these 20,000 men and horses takes every tenth horse and man. The whole country is to be put into classes of 10 saddlehorses each and one of these is to be lotted for the cavalry, both horse and master. It is thought that this affair will cost those that have one saddlehorse £5 each as it is supposed that a man and a horse will cost £50.

December – A Bill has been passed by the Parliament of this Kingdom for the raising of 15,000 men for the Army and Navy, to be raised by the county, viz from the taxed houses according to the number and Wyresdale, Slyne and Hest have to fund two men. The number of houses in Wyresdale that is taxed is 83, in Slyne and Hest are only 37 so Wyresdale will have to find a man and to pay something more than one third the price towards another which will be a heavy burden upon the people to be paid and collected the same way that the poor rates are.

On the 3rd Decr the Wyresdale people with those of Slyne and Hest hired two men for the Navy, one called John Dilworth for £25 4s and the other for £24 3s. The latter was an inhabitant of Garstang with a wife and two children and another in great forwardness. John Dilworth has been hired before for Garstang for £20 but they refusing him a billet and he thinking he could get more offered himself again and was hired by Wyresdale people. Both of the men was sworn in and part of their money paid them, about £8 or £9 each in hand, the rest to be paid when they went on Shipboard. These two men cost the Township £49, 7s in Bounty money besides a great deal spent about hiring them. I suppose there was spent about £3 or £4 as there was many of them and they drank very hard.

Estimate as to value of Thomas Bateson's higher ground: -

The rent offered for this farm is about 33 or 34 acres was £36 but Thomas Bateson wanted £38 and the tenant was to mow $4^1/_2$ acres and to plough 7 acres per year, leaving $11^1/_2$ acres for pasture. We will suppose 1 horse = 2 gails and 2 Cows = 2 gails[33] 4 stirks[34] 2 gails + 4 Twenters[35] nearly 3 gails = in all 9 gails. Corn will make per year 4 kinfull [*sic*] each year at 5 loads of Meal

That is 20 loads at 30/- per load = £30
2 Cows to make £5 of each 10
4 heifers to sell each year 40
= 80.0.0.
Expenditure. There will be besides the rent
3 Stirks to buy each year £10
Clearing of the place per year 5
Rent bid 36
= 51.0.0.
= 29.0.0.

Decr 12th: – About 3 weeks ago the wife of Wm Clarkson of Hathornthwaite vaccary being in a very poor state of health as she has been for many years but somewhat worse than usual for some months past two girls went to visit her and she was sitting by the fire, and she not being able to stir much about, she desired the girls to go upstairs and make the bed, which they not readily complying with she rather scowled at them so that they went and when they were gone she got up about something out of her chair and being subject to fainting fits she fainted and fell into the fire where she laid for some time before the girls knew of her dreadful situation. When they came downstairs they found her so most dreadfully burnt that they did not expect her surviving but she is alive at this time though not expected to recover. Her gown and stays were burnt off her back.

The Navy men hired for Wyresdale, Slyne and Hest will cost us in all about £52 10s with expenses, so Wyresdale's share will be £36.6.3.

In Ellel they have hired two men at about £30 or £31, 10s each.

It is thought the Cavalry Bill will not get forward in the form it now is in nobody understanding it. The Ministry talk of making another Act to explain the first. The Quaker's bill sticks in the House of Lords and is put off from one time till another.

---

33 Or gale, rent on a plot of land.
34 Young bullock or heifer.
35 Or twinter, two-year old cattle.

Lord Malmesbury, the English ambassador at Paris makes no progress in making peace, neither side being it appears sufficiently humbled yet.

Our government amuse us with talking about the French invading this nation, but I think it is only a scheme to make this nation raise more men and more money. Our government I think are our worst enemies. They aim at having all and they will have all if we will submit to all they would impose upon us. But Pitt has found out a new mode of Finance viz that every one shall subscribe a fifth part of their income for the use of the next year to be paid again in 4 years with interest at 5 percent. There is £25,000,000 to be raised in this way instead of a Loan.

A letter had been received from John Richmond out of America and he likes very well. He has purchased 144 statute acres of very good land for something more than £600 of English money. The estate he has bought is near a town called Pakepoy about 90 miles north of New York on the East side of Hudson's river which is navigable above a hundred miles further than Pakepoy.

George Parker has bought an Estate somewhere near to John Richmond's and he wants men as servants to go over. He will give them £15 a year and pay for their passage, but whether he means English or New York currency is not known. An English guinea will pay £1/17 at New York.

Conditions as to letting a Farm.

Decr 13th: – Yesterday my father took Thomas Bateson's Higher Ground all but the old field house gardens. The conditions are:

Rent £36 p.a. the term 3 years. The tenant to clear half of Thomas Bateson's whole estate to the Poor Rate and to pay half the Land Tax. The Moles according to the number of acres. The Landlord to fence the old Field round. John Bateson to have manure for his garden. The Tenant to have the Ash midden from the house. Thomas Bateson to have permission to lead away several heaps of mould cast upon the Bent. Thomas Bateson to have permission to turn his Beasts out until towards the time that grass comes. Timothy Cragg to have the same permission at the term end. The manure found on coming to be set where the tenant pleases. The 1st and 2nd years all the manure to be set in the Meadow & in the 3rd year to be left in the fold.

The people of Wyresdale, Slyne and Hest hired two men for the navy. One was a Garstang man and the other was called John Dilworth and he was hired by Garstang people for a navy man at £20 before the time. But at the time they were to be raised Wyresdale people hired him and got him sworn in and then Garstang people were vexed and came and took Dilworth from Lancaster and put him in the House of Correction at Preston and so it was noised in the country that Wyresdale people had lost their man and Ellel folk were very full of it because they were vexed that Wyresdale folk had hired men for less money than they could do. Upon these reports Joshua Bibby the Constable went to Lancaster to the High Constable and made him acquainted with it and he said that Garstang folk had no business with the man seeing he was hired and sworn in that they would go to the regulating Captain and see what must be done. So they went and the Captain sent Joshua to Garstang to acquaint that if they did not set Dilworth at liberty they would be proceeded against according to Law so Joshua went and told them and they said not much to him but wanted to know something about paying the expence of putting the man in the House of Correction.

Decr 18th. Today Wm Kelsall's youngest son was buried at Wyresdale Meeting. He died of the small pox aged 14 years. The small pox is very rife at this time through the country and of the worst kind. In Garstang they are very mortal and nearly one half die. There were 4 neighbours there with 2 children each and they each lost one and the other got very finely through. At Galgate a young woman aged 22 died of the small pox a few days since.

1797

January 11th: – The small pox very general in Wyresdale both natural and also by inoculation. All do well by inoculation as yet.

The New Militia to be raised are to be balloted for on the 23rd of this month at Lancaster. It takes 1 man out of 10 that are liable to serve. In Wyresdale there will be 7 to raise and in Ellel 14¹/₂ men will be wanted and in Quernmore it is said 7. In lower Wyresdale 5 which are polled. In Cleveley there was 14 liable to serve and they were put to another Township and 2 out of Cleveley were polled.

On the 18th the men in Wyresdale met at the Chapel to enter into a club and subscribe money for to raise the new militia men and about 60 entered that day. They subscribed half a guinea each man.

On 23rd the people of Lonsdale Hundred were balloted for at Lancaster. Wyresdale had to fund 7 and the lots fell as follows: -
myself, David Cragg;
Rich Birkett of Bagman House, hatter;
Roy Knowles of the Moorhead, hatter;
Rob Clarkson of the Cawlonge, mason;
Thomas Broadley at the Borderside, farmer;
George Drinkall of Marshaw, farmer;
William Simpson of Tarnbrook, shoemaker.

There is already several men hired as subscribers for Wyresdale, both in Wyresdale and at other places at £8, 13s each.

January 30th: – Notice has been given to the Constables to put off any further proceedings about the Supplementary Militia for a month.

Servant men are very dear this year and are now about from £11 to £13 per year each, but at this day men will hire at one place and if anybody afterwards offer them a few shillings more wages they will sent the first master word to look out for another man for they will not come.

Now when wheat is cheap the shopkeepers sell us more than 5¹/₂ lbs of the best flour for a shilling and 6¹/₂ lbs of seconds. Last year about the same time wheat was between 60/- and 70/- per load and flour was made all of one sort and was sold at $3^3/4$ lb for a shilling. I believe there is 5/- spent in flour this month for 1/- in the same month last year.

The cotton and woollen trades are most exceedingly bad and low. Scarcely worth following but that people in such trades cannot turn themselves to any other branch of trade.

February: – The 4th of this month was an appeal day at Lancaster about the horse tax, that is of pleasure horses for the purchase of riding and several at Wyresdale thought to appeal but they being called up and Jos Whiteside appealing and he could not get off unless he would swear that he never rode to any other place than the church or market. The business of appealing was carried on thus: –

When they went before the Court the person appealing was sworn to answer whatever questions he should be asked and a shilling was demanded which he was forced to pay before he should be examined. They would not speak to him before he paid 1/-. When the shilling was paid he was asked how much land he farmed and whether he rode to, and then he was asked if he never during the last year rode to see any friend or relation or went away to any distant fair, which he had done sometimes so he could not get off and the rest seeing his fate did not appeal and so saved their shillings and submitted to this arbitrary tax, which in my opinion does not extend to farmers by the true meaning of the Act, but the Justices in this Country are overbearing and oppressive men and strain the Laws beyond their proper bounds.

Feb 18th: – Ortner Wood was sold at Lancaster this night. A deal of company was there and the whole was sold together to Matthew Butler and Joseph Whiteside for the sum of £699 to be paid on the 1st February 1798. All the wood to be cut down and carried away before 13th Feb 1798.

Feb 28th: – Every kind of trade is dull and a great number of hands turned out of employ in the cotton trade and many bankruptcys have taken place.

March 2nd: – the supplementary militia were sworn in today at Lancaster. Richard Birkett of the Bagman house in Wyresdale was one that was balloted to serve in the supplementary militia and he being one called a Quaker though not in unity with Friends, but he either through poverty or conscience refused to enter into the Club, and when he was balloted he did not hire a substitute nor intended to serve himself and he appeared at the time and place of swearing in and when he was called upon he refused to swear and had no substitute so the justices threatened to grant a warrant to claim his goods, which will undoubtedly be the case if he do not sign over his effects to the benefit of his creditors and if so then he will be imprisoned for some time.

March 8th: – A fast and prayer day by order of Government to implore the Almighty to assist them – that is the English – to kill and murder all the French and conquer France.

March 10th: – There is much talk about this time about the French invading this nation which our Government seems to fear they will do and great consternation prevails through the Country, but for my part, though I think they may come if they please, yet I am none afraid of them, nor no men has need to fear but those that live in ease, plenty and luxury and tyrannise over the poor people for let the French come and set up what sort of Government they please it cannot well be worse than ours is at this time. But only a little time since the French landed about 1400 galley slaves and convicts on the coast of Wales which have been taken prisoners as they were put on shore without any arms to defend themselves with if they had had a mind so to do.

There is another thing that has caused alarm and that is the bank of England has stopped payment. They will cash no more Bills. What will be the consequence of this is not known but it is supposed that very soon there will be no money left and all payments will be made in paper which is unfortunately worth nothing.

The Quakers' tithe bill has passed the House of Commons. There was a division on the 3rd reading & there appeared for the Bill passing into a Law 33 against it 33 therefore the Members being equal the Speaker gave his casting vote in favour of the Quakers. It is thought it will not pass the House of Lords. Note: It was only the 2nd reading of the Bill and there was sometime after a motion made for the Bill being read that day 6 months which was done accordingly and so the Bill was lost.

March 25th: – There was a very large Ox shown at Lancaster today, supposed to be the largest ever seen in England. The property of John Ibbelson of Bedale in Yorkshire. It is rising 7 years old and is $6^3/_4$ yds long, 6 yds round his chest 19 hands high $12^1/_2$ ft from his cheek to his Buttock, 5 ft 6 in from the top of his shoulder to his Bresket 3 ft 2 in between his hips and weight upwards of 2 Tons 5 cwt 8 lbs. I gave 3d to see this Beast.

The Assizes begun at Lancaster this day when 16 prisoners were to take their trial for various offences besides a number of causes to be determined this Assize about various trivial affairs.

April: – On the 3rd of this month there was a man hanged at Lancaster for murder & Robbery near Bolton le Moors.

On the 1st one Middleton of Liverpool was tried at Lancaster on a charge of wilfully setting fire to a warehouse which was burnt down and several more adjoining homes and many lives lost. The trial continued till 11 o'clock at night and the Jury after deliberating about half an hour brought in a verdict of not guilty. It is said the whole Court believed he was guilty. There were 4 Barristers employed against him and he had 3.

April 8th: – Came on to be tried today at Lancaster a case between John Blackburn, plaintiff and John Gaskell, defendant about a footpath through plaintiffs and defendants fields. The ground and path in dispute is at the side of the river Conder near Ellel Chapel. When one goes from Galgate to the Wardhouses they pass over the Conder over a footbridge and into a field on a path which in a few roads turns into the lane again to the Wardhouses and this disputed path when we get over the Bridge in the field (this field belongs to the defendant Croskell) this path turns to the left down the field and a small corner of it and then goes into the plaintiff's fields. The plea was that there was no road there, but that the defendant places a stile in his own fence into the plaintiff's field where no stile had ever been before & this stile induced people to have 1 that way. There was only 2 evidences examined on the plaintiffs side viz John Gardner, Mason, & Thos Harrison & they proved nothing but that they had frequently gone that way themselves at all times of the year. The plaintiff was non-suited.

May: – The most conversation at this time is about a mutiny on board the fleet at Spithead and at St Helena the whole of the common sailors being combined together for the redress of grievances which they labour under.[36] They received orders to put to sea and instead of that every man refused and not one ship weighed anchor but every ships crew chose two delegates each who met together and transacted business for the whole crews. The grievances they complained of were too little wages, too little meal etc. and they therefore demanded an increase of wages from 22/6 per month to 28/- and 16oz to the lb of meal instead of 12 oz as before and a more equal distribution of prize money, and not to be whipped by any tyrannical petty officer on little or no real offence and to be pardoned for this affair. And an Act of Parliament passed granting these things.

Most of these things were granted, their wages raised to 28/- per month and 16oz to the lb of meal and a free pardon by the Kings Proclamation but no Act of Parliament brought forward but all was quiet and tranquil on board the whole fleet. On the 7th or 8th of this month an express came for the fleet to sail immediately but not a single ship moved and the delegates from the different ships came to London of 90 guns[37] and Admiral Colpoise refused to let them come on board and told them that if they come on board and told them that if they in the least attempted to mutiny he would fire upon them. The sailors insisted the delegates should come on board. The Admiral ordered the Marines aft and ordered them to fire which some of them did and others grounded their arms and 3 or 4 of the sailors were wounded. The sailors then got arms and fired on the officers and killed one and wounded several more and the delegates got on board & put the Admiral in irons etc and it is said he will be tried by a Court Martial of the Common Sailors and other accounts say he was to be hanged or shot the day after. The greatest consternation prevails. The reason for this second mutiny is that there is no bill brought forward in Parliament granting what was before promised and they did not think themselves safe without an Act being passed in their favour.

June 9th: – The mutinous sailors at Spithead and St Helena are pacified and put to sea but there has a more dreadful disaffection taken place on the river Thames and Medway among the sailors at Sheerness and Chatham and the river. They insisted upon terms quite out of reason it is said and their grievances cannot be settled. The government will not grant them what they want and all intercourse is stopped in the river. The sailors plunder every ship that comes up or down the river and the batteries along the river are manned and furnaces in readiness to heat red hot to fire at the ships if the Mutineers make an attempt to sail and yesterday

36 See A. T. Patterson, *The Naval Mutiny at Spithead, 1797* (Portsmouth, Portsmouth City Council, 1968).
37 HMS London, 90 guns.

I heard that Parliament was passing a Bill declaring the Mutineers to be out of the Kings protection and that they were traitors and pirates and should be reduced by force. There is over 20 ships of war in this mutiny, 8 or 9 of them being ships of the line. I suppose there is between 7000 & 8000 men & it is a question whether the other fleets will fight them. It is likely enough for this fleet to sail away and deliver themselves up to France.

July: – There is a new budget of taxes brought forth which will lie pretty hard on some people. There is to be 3/- additional on workhorses making 5/- per workhorse & next he proposes a tax of 2/6 per piece on silver or metal watches & 10/- on gold ones & 5/- per piece for clocks so we must pay for knowing how the time comes out.

On the 21st was buried at Forton Chapel Richard Ashburn of Lower Wyresdale opposite Cleveley Mill, he having been a cripple for many years being hurt in a marl pit. He could not walk at all but rode in a cart and went to Lancaster almost every week since I can remember where he would drive into any part of the town and transact business of any sort and make his market. He constantly employed himself in making Bee Hives and covering rollers for Scorton factory folk, thereby earning much money. He had a farm under Lord Archibald Hamilton which by his death is out of Lease, it being the second farm that is out of lease by due cause of nature under Lord A. Hamilton. It is said that somebody had been at the steward before my Uncle died to take the farm which to some may seem strange but which I believe is true.

July 24th: – Yesterday John Field and John Albright from Lancaster were at our house on a visit I having requested to become a member among the Quakers.

August 1st: – The newspapers give account of very dreadful storms of Lightning and Thunder and much hurt having been done thereby in many parts of England about the middle of last month.

August: – The duty or Tax upon watches commences the 5th day of this month. The tax is 2/6 per watch. Servants employed in husbandry are exempted.

Dolphinholme Factory Weir at the commencement of this Company taking the Factory underhand about 2 years ago was made low and very firm and was thought to be so perfect as to stand a long time, but almost every flood did it some damage and now the tail of the Weir, all the planks, are so smashed & crushed and battered by the Water, stones and Ice falling upon them that they are quite done, so last winter the Proprietors seeing the damaged state of the tail of the Weir resolved to have it replaced with stone which was last week laid down, that is, all the tail but there is yet a – [38] to be raised up with Ashlar Stones to the top of the Weir, but at present it cannot be done by reason of the water being too high.

August 14th: – A great flood in the Wyre which washed Dolphinholme Factory weir entirely down, every bit of it bodily together and nothing is left but the stone trail of the Weir which was put in lately. The reason of the weir being washed

---

38   Here Cragg inserted a symbol of a line followed by a semicircle.

away is this, there was a small space left between the new tail of the Weir and the Weir and the Water falling off the Weir with inconceivable violence wrought down the space and undermined the Weir and blew it up all together and now the water runs along its old course undisturbed. The factory is of course stopped and great numbers of hands are employed in erecting a temporary weir till one more substantial can be made and the waters lower. This weir was thought to be so firm and well finished as to stand a long time but in the course of than less than 2 years after many considerable damages had been sustained and repaired is now entirely swept away so headstrong & impatient of obstruction is this river Wyre.

September: – The Assizes ended at Lancaster on the 2nd of this month and there was 20 crown prisoners tried, 6 of which were acquitted.

October: – On the 16th of this month George Bibby of the Lee being at Lancaster and was loading a pack of wool into a Cart at the Bear & Staff yard. He was on the top of the cart and pulling up at the Woolpack and the Ostler was lifting below and as George was pulling as hard as he could his hands slipped their hold and he fell backwards off the cart and light on the pavement and was dreadfully hurt. His arm was broken between his hand and elbow in one place and his shoulder put out and his collar bone broken and the cup of his shoulder broken. Rawlinson the bone setter was at the Bear & Staff at the time and set his arm and put his shoulder in but by reason of the cup being broken he put it in 3 times before it would bide. The Bone setter thought he would be able to go home the day after.

At the end of the month the newspapers give an account that there has been extremely heavy rains in Ireland which has done incredible damage to the crops on the lowlands and in England the wet weather has done great damage in the corn especially that which was forward.

The tax on clocks and watches is unproductive all clocks in houses with no more than 6 windows are exempted from the tax. There is only 9 clocks entered in Wyresdale.

Cawthorne the tyrant of this neighbourhood has mostly this summer been kept prisoner in his own house he is not daring to stir out of fear of Bailiffs except on the first day of the week when he commonly was out; but now since Michaelmas he has been often out and showing his despotical authority over the poor country people. The reason of his being at liberty is said to be that all the writs against him are out, the term being ended. He is an uncommon man, one would have thought when he was cashiered for an officer with such infamy and then turned out of the Parliament House, his affairs in such confusion as to be forced to sign over his effects, one would have thought all this would have humbled him and made him a peaceable man, but instead of that I think he is worse and worse.

Oct 21st: – News came this week of Admiral Duncan defeating the Dutch Fleet on the coast of Holland taking 9 men of war and 2 Frigates after a severe engagement in which many men were killed and wounded.[39]

---

39 Battle of Camperdown, 11 October 1797.

Catshaw Factory – This Factory which has been stopped for some years, I believe about 3 years, was let this summer to a Mr Taylor of Manchester for a term of years. All the wheels to be taken at a fair valuation. 3 men came some months ago to put things in order and boarded at Wm Holkinson's and they employed some families in cleaning & putting things in order and when they should have paid them ran away and it was reported that Taylor was a Bankrupt. So those employed thought they had lost all their work, but about 3 weeks ago Taylor came and the Factory started again. So now all the Factory's [*sic*] in this Country are got to work again.

Cawthorne sold land about Skerton a few days ago for £2000. The Grapes Inn in Lancaster belonging to Cawthorne was offered for sale and about £350 bid but was not sold. They set it up at £500. Cawthorne's debt is £59,000.

A few days ago Peter Tomlinson received a summons from Justice Bradshaw to appear before him at Lancaster on the 28th of this month and answer the charge brought against him for carrying a gun in a certain field in quest of game without licence the penalty being £20. So accordingly Peter attended taking with him Joseph Whiteside & some others, particularly Rd Huntington, who saw the affair of taking the gun. Thomas Stone met them before the Justice as the whole evidence against Peter and gave an account of the transaction and of Peter being very saucy. Peter said he was in the footpath and was saucy only in his own vindication. The Justice handed a book to Thomas Stone to swear that Peter was out of the Path but Thomas would not swear that but threw the book down so the Justice told him it was over with him and asked Peter if he had any person to give evidence that he was in the path and he had he said four or five. The Justice told him one was sufficient and he picked upon Rd Huntington who could not then be found so it was referred to that day week when Rd Huntington is to appear.

Peter Tomlinson appeared on the 4th November at Lancaster with Rd Huntington and Richard's evidence cleared Peter of all blame. Thos Stone was there and he would have sworn anything but the Justices would not hearken to him. He offered to swear that Rd Huntington was half a mile off when the affair happened but was not suffered.

November: – Died on the 18th of this month at an advanced age William Markin of Lower Wyresdale after an illness of about 3 weeks. He was at Lentworth sale the 30th of last month in perfect health but as he went home from the sale he complained of a pain in his back which he thought he could cover with his finger end but it increased and spread over his whole body and he was exceedingly full of pain during the time of his last illness. He is to be buried at Wyresdale Chapel the 20th of this month.

Lancaster canal: – November 24th: – Today was a great rejoicing day and much ado made on opening the Lancaster Canal when the first barge load of coals came from Preston to Lancaster and a barge loaded with limestone from Borwick. The Canal is now opened from Preston to Borwick or further and beyond Preston it is open for many miles from the far end to this side of Chorley on which an abundance of coals and cannel are carried to about 7 miles beyond Preston and are carried on the canal about 7 miles. A barge loaded with coals was sunk at Garstang on the 22nd in consequence of the storm of wind which made the water rough and the barge being heavy laden it kept dibbing & dibbing till it sunk.

December: – On the 6th Cawthorne's land at Lower Starbank and the Crag in Ellel should have been sold at Galgate but not many people appearing the sale was put off to a future period. On the 5th all Cawthorne's possessions in the Stakehouses was sold at the Oakenclough for about £1100. Richard Topin bought 2 shares. Roger Kenron 1 share or lot. Richard Jackson 1 lot & Lawson's steward 1 lot. All the Stakehouses Vaccary belongs to different persons in a very extraordinary manner. There is not I believe one farm in it that belongs to one and only one landlord. Cawthorne's part made about £35 per year. In some farms he claimed one half, in others a fourth, an eighth, a sixteenth, a thirty-second or a sixty-fourth part. Richard Topin bought one Lot which brought in 5s 6d per year, gave £50 which is too much by half or more. There was a great company and the sale cost between £9 & £10 in drink.

The affair about Peter Tomlinson and his gun is very much talked of all along ever since the first and he having come off clear as before said. Now sometime since Lord Archibald heard of the affair and Robert Mitchinson his steward sent for Peter and Joseph Whiteside to come down to him. So they went at Garstang Fair the 22nd of last month and related to him the whole affair. Joseph was desirous of letting the affair rest but the steward would acquaint Lord Archibald with the affair and about a week since Lord Archibald sent for Peter to come down to Ashton Hall and he went accordingly and related the whole affair again to Justice Clayton. It is thought by many that Cawthorne will be proceeded against for robbery, it being felony to take anything from a man in the highway but I am afraid it will all come to nothing.

There is to be a Thanksgiving Prayer day the 19th of this month throughout Great Britain for the victory over the Dutch fleet the 11 of October and all other naval victorys since the commencement of this glorious and necessary (bloody and pompous) war and the King will go in great pomp and parade to St Paul's cathedral and hear the Thanksgiving Prayer there:
"Cease ye fools and go no further
God requires no thanks for murder".

We have great reason to be thankful indeed, for only in the action with the Dutch Fleet on the 11 of October the English had upwards of 300 killed and 700 wounded. We must needs be very thankful for these 700 cripples who perhaps may go a begging all the remainder of their days would to God but that the Authors of this war did but experience the hardships of these poor fellows. These men – those heaven born ministers of ours – feel no hardships. They rest in ease and luxury and the cries of the wounded and maimed reach not their ears, nor the lamentations of the wives and children of the slain.

Decr 19th: – This is the Thanksgiving Prayer day by order of the Government. It was but badly observed in this country. There were not many people at the chapel.

The newspapers are much taken up with the trial of Captain Williamson of the Agincourt man of war for negligence cowardice and disaffection in action on the 11th October with the Dutch fleet. He had no men killed or wounded. We have an account of 11 days trial already.

It is reported in the papers that a third part of the Supplementary Militia are to be called up immediately viz 20,000 men. The principle subject of conversation at this time is a bill now pending in Parliament to triple the assessed taxes. A man who now pays 3 guineas assessed taxes will be called upon to pay 9 guineas more making the whole 12 guineas. These triple assessed taxes go but badly down in London and most other places but the Bill is not yet passed. It has been read twice and was to be committed on the 18th of this month and to be read a third time as soon as possible after as our Heaven born ministers were anxious to have it passed before the Christmas Holy Days. It was to undergo many modifications in Committee and made so as to bear lightly on the lower and middle classes of the people and lie mostly on those that are able to pay.

Decr 23rd: – Last week Cawthorne left Wyreside and is gone out of this country. It is said for a few weeks only.

Lancaster canal. Lancaster Canal which was opened on the 22nd of November and since that time several barge load of coals and cannel have been brought to Lancaster and Galgate from Savok[40] a little below Preston and they are sold at Lancaster at 1/- per cwt for cannel and 18 per cwt for coals but it must be observed that only 112 lbs is allowed to a hundredweight which is 8 lbs less than is usual and customary in this country. Edmund Jackson of Galgate was a captain of a barge but has now thrown up the business for he was himself and a lad and a horse and was allowed only 30/- a week which is too little.

There is limekilns already built in various parts along the sides of the Canal more than will be of any use anytime soon for it seems very improbable that a sufficient quantity of coals can be had to supply the country with in any moderate time for all the coals that now come along the Canal are first brought down the Douglas and then up the Ribble and landed below Preston and these taken into the Canal barges and until a communication is made over the Ribble at Preston between the two ends of the Canal there will not be any great plenty of coals for the country, much less for burning lime. It has been talked that both ends of the canal will be brought as near to the Ribble at Preston or Walton Bridge and into the other end a distance of about a quarter of a mile. If this be done it will make a very throng [sic] place over Walton Bridge, but this method is only to be pursued until such time as an acquaduct is made over the Ribble which it is computed will cost the sum of £60,000.

Political affairs: – There is not much that need be said upon this head except in the line of new taxes and new impositions upon the people, but this new fangled way of raising 8 millions of money for the service of the ensuing year is a

40 Salwick, five miles west of Preston?

matter that occasions a great deal of conversation. The ministers [*sic*] scheme is to double, tripple, quadruple and quintuple the assessed taxes – All those who pay less than 20/- are exempted. Between 20/- and 40/- to pay half a rate and so on. The Act is not yet passed but those who pay between £40 and £50 assessed taxes are to be quadrupled, that is a man who now pays £40 must pay £200 and those who pay £50 will be quintupled and so must pay £300. If it gets forward in this proposed manner a better tax could not be laid for it lies upon those that are able to pay and is a very likely way to bring about a peace. Charles Gibson of Quernmore Park now pays about £100 assessed taxes and if the new tax takes place he will have £600 to pay.

Col. Cawthorne of Wyreside now pays about £46 and will have to pay £230, which is a deal to pay when a man is worth nothing and perhaps £10,000 worse than nothing. Several others will feel the weight of this tax which is to continue only during the war or little longer. Pitt said that farmer's [*sic*] horses he did not mean should be included in the assessed taxes but thought that the farmers could not think it hard if they were doubled. If this be the case farmers work horses will be 12/- per year they being 6/- per year at this time. This is the consequence of an unjust and unnecessary war and which will involve all Europe in ruin.

The French have made a calculation that the English and other nations that have engaged France this war have lost 2,773,000 men. What effusion of human blood has been shed for the purpose of setting up a King in France. I think the English Constitution in its present form cannot subsist many years longer. We are so much involved in Debt, have so much interest to pay for this Debt that the nation groans under the continual accumulating burdens that are laid upon them. If the French do come and invade this land as they are threatening to do I think it would be no difficult task to conquer this nation. However when the French do come they will wipe off all old chalks at once. But the French are not come yet nor I believe do intend to come. They only mean to keep us in a continual alarm and make us keep a very strong force up and thereby ruin us by expense, which I believe will soon be the case. This government is on the high road to destruction. Parliament is but a name, the Minister rules them at his will and whatever method, whatever law he proposes, he carries it through the parliament with a great majority of votes – all Place men and Pensioners – for no other vote has he.

The Pleasure Horse tax of 10/- each horse for the purpose of riding was the only tax that ever this country stickled to pay cheerfully, but most farmers in this country thinking themselves not liable to the tax were many years and did not pay it, until last year our honest Justices for the hundred of Lonsdale found out that every farmer who farmed £70 per year and every man that had an estate worth £35 per annum was liable also and at this time the tax was raised to 21/- per year. Several people appealed against this tax but very few got off.

The tax on farmers work horses went down without an if,[41] all under 13 hands being exempted.

---

41 i.e. without objection.

The tax on dogs was swallowed readily, all that paid no assessed taxes being exempt.

The tax on clocks and watches almost totally evaded in this country.

The triple assessed Tax if it gets forward will not affect the people in Wyresdale much for most of them pay less than 20/- a year assessed taxes.

It is now 5 years since the commencement of this war, begun with a view to conquer France and now carried on only to gain a good and honourable peace which yet cannot be done, neither side are sufficiently humbled nay indeed the French are much elated to make peace or have conquered their dominions and made new Republics round them.

The people of Great Britain will have to pay in taxes and parochial rates this next year £34,000,000 which is said to be more than ever was paid before by £10,000,000. The Triple Assessed Tax is to be laid on for 2 years and a quarter to let our enemies see that our resources are not yet exhausted. The Stamp Duty is so high that there are not more than one-fourth of the Almanacs published this year, they being now 1/4 each.

On the 28th was buried at Wyresdale Chapel James Bibby of Marshaw aged about 74 years, he had been afflicted with the Scurvy which at last brought him to the grave. His month and throat were so much afflicted that he could not eat, but lived on fluids alone and at last he could not take that and it is probably he died of want being able to take nothing.

1798

January: – On 23rd of this month was buried at Wyersdale Chapel William Stone of the Abystead, gamekeeper under JF Cawthorne for a great number of years. A savage, tyrannic overbearing man. Illnatured, curst and wicked. Beloved nor respected by no man but I believe was glad he was called from his works to receive his reward. He sorely repented of his illspent life a little before he died, and confessed he had been guilty of every kind of sin whatever but murder and told what a good life he would lead if he recovered again, far different from what he had before done, but it is to be feared that had he been restored again to health he would have been the old man again. He died of a consumption and had been visibly going for some years, yet he was as rough and turbulent and as wicked as ever, even till he could be so no longer. It is said that he sharply reproved John Drinkall for swearing a few weeks before he died. So he is gone to his reward. May his worthy master soon follow, for he has done enough.

All trade is exceedingly bad and worse and worse, occasioned by the war and now more particularly by the French prohibiting the import of any English goods into France by any means which is a terrible blow to the English manufacture of all denominations. The cotton trade is sunk to the lowest ebb. The hatting trade exceedingly bad. The triple assessed tax Bill passed. Farmers horses now 18/- each if he farms £70 per year or upwards.

The Supplementary Militia to be embodied very soon & also the Cavalry men.

The French threaten to invade this land. Our governors pretend to be alarmed and actually invade our pockets and purses. What else will the French have need of but all that we have.

On the 20th of January Isaac Dobson son of Joseph Dobson of Quernmore was at Lancaster and he tarried late at night and got beeryfied [*sic*] as is often the case with him though not 20 years of age. He was drinking at the Boar's Head, Thomas Edmondsons, till about 11 o'clock at night and then set off towards home and was taken up the Moor Lane and over the Canal Bridge by some acquaintance and so came forward and as he came down Conder Bridge a man on horseback met with him and dismounted his horse and knocked Isaac Dobson down with an Iron Bar and then robbed him of his money viz five shillings and left him sprawling on the road. Isaacs face was much bruised and his tongue split and his throat hurt so that when he got him [in] he could not talk and a Doctor was sent for immediately. This is the fair side of the story; now for the black side. A man who lives at the Well House being in bed waked sometime of the night and heard his horse go out of the stable but did not get up just them [*sic*], but towards morning he could not be easy and got up and his horse was come again but was lamed so that he was forced to take it to the Farrier and as his horse and Isaac Dobson both had need of a surgeon most folk thought that they had both been hurt together. That Isaac had taken the horse out of the stable and ridden it towards home as hard as he could and that it had fallen and so hurt both itself and Isaac and that is the general opinion at this time. The horse had a cloth on it and a sursingle about it and the cloth was found in Conder Brow and the sursingle was found at this side of the new mill off the road at a place where they pass over a slack or gutter, and it is a very rough stony place and there the sursingle was found and also have on the stones that had come off the horse and some drops of blood thereabouts a proof good enough that the accident happened there. But Dobson's folk set forth a dreadful story of Isaac's being robbed and that it was an Irishman that robbed him who works about Lancaster and Isaac says he had a good deal of money and was afraid of being robbed and so he left it at Lancaster and that was the reason he had such a small sum about him. Now Joseph Dobson his father being at Lancaster sometime after the robbery took place, was in a public company and the Irishman, the reputed thief, was in the same room also and Joseph Dobson spoke up and said 'that is the man that robbed my son;' the man denied the fact and could prove himself in another place if necessary, but the Irishman went to an attorney and set him to work immediately for scandalising him and in a little time it would have been run up to a great sum for costs, but the Irishman stopped the attorney a piece to see if Joseph Dobson would make it up but Joseph was too stupid for that, but his wife went and made up the affair with the attorney and paid £5 for damages and the costs of suit about £2. The Irishman and 2 or 3 of his companions went to the Public House with the £5 and never left it till the whole was spent. Joseph Dobson rubs his arm and says when they have got it it is nought. The wounds that Isaac received required the attendance of a surgeon several times and it is said cost £3 so the whole affair is said to have cost Joseph Dobson the sum of £10.

February: – JF Cawthorne the petty tyrant of this Country has advertised a quantity of wood to be sold on the 14th of this month and he has marked some trees along his own fence which divides his land from Lord Archibalds and some he marked that grew from 3 to 6 feet from his fence in Lord Archibald's field because he thought he had a right to make a back dyke & so the trees would some be in the Dyke bottom and some in the Dyke breast but Mitchison getting to know he and Joseph Jackson and Richard Robinson came to view the trees in question and some the steward marked over again as belonging to Lord Archibald and others he set down doubtfull and Cawthorne came to them and wanted them to mark some that were in the fence but these they would not meddle.

The Militia which was balloted 5 years ago their time being up this winter and so they ought to be discharged but it is said that those who were hired as substitutes at that time must not be discharged but must serve during the war. Those who were balloted and served for themselves have been discharged and others balloted in their place. Now in Wyresdale 2 men were polled and both hired substitutes and both substitutes are continued on and so Wyresdale is not called upon for any more men on that account. Ellel is the same. It seems hard that these men should serve perhaps twice as long as they thought of, at the same time it seems an easement to the townships who hired substitutes but in reality it is not much advantage to Wyresdale for they hired a man with a family and have 3/- per week to pay for maintenance these 5 years.

Feb 26th – Something more than a week ago some men were drinking in a Public House in Preston and they differed about drink healths to the King, Queen and John Horrocks. They talked to such a degree that one man a bookbinder was so provoked and mad that he declared he would be revenged of some of them. From the Public House they went into the street and there a desperate battle begun. The bookbinder pulled out a two-edged knife and stabbed one man into the belly so that his entrails came out and he died in about 2 hours, another man he stabbed and he died immediately, and a third was wounded in the arm, it is said in disarming the barbarian. The man that begun the quarrel ran away unhurt. The Bookbinder was secured and is brought to Lancaster Castle to take his trial at the next assizes.

About the beginning of this month Peter Tomlinson went again to Robert Mitchison and talked about his affair with Cawthorne and a few days after Cawthorne sent Joseph Whiteside his gun back again. John Jackson of Greenbank took it and went to Joseph Whiteside who was thrashing in the barn. John told him that Mr Cawthorne had sent him his gun again and gave him leave to shoot crows or anything else, but Joseph refused to take the gun, for he was instructed so to do by the Justice Clayton so John Jackson reared the gun up to the barn side and left it and there it is yet. A few days after that Peter was summoned by R Mitchison to attend on him again and after some conversation he sent Peter to Justice Clayton, Blackburn, whither Peter went & was almost a week away and came back about the 20th of this month. Cawthorne writ a letter to Fanshaw, Lord of Hashaw [*sic*], a long account of his steward's conduct, what a sad fellow he was and wished him to be turned out of his place, but it appears that Fanshaw did not give credit to Cawthorne's complaint for he sent the letter to Tomlinson his steward, at Garstang.

In the first week of March Lord Archibald sent for Peter Tomlinson to come to Ashton Hall which he did and was charged whatever he did not to make the affair up with Cawthorne, but if Cawthorne came to him for that purpose he must tell him to go to Justice Clayton. Joseph Whiteside told my father as a great secret that they were proceeding against Cawthorne and have retained a councillor at London to come to Lancaster and it is to be tried this Assizes and it is thought Cawthorne will be tried for robbery. It was said that there was £50 expences already on the plaintiff's side – that is Peter Tomlinson's – but it may be observed that Peter is a very poor man a day labourer with a large family so will be as able to pay £1000 as £10. His backers must stand the rubber.

At the Lancaster assizes holden about the latter end of March a bill of indictment was found against Cawthorne and Thomas Stone for assaulting Peter Tomlinson and Cawthorne and Thos Stone was bound in 2 sureties each to appear at the next assizes at Lancaster where they are to take their trial. John Jackson, Cawthorne's steward and Robert Banton of Wyreside were bound with Thos Stone in £20 each and R Jonson, New Street, and Lawyer Baldwin were bound with Cawthorne. Cawthorne and Stone were extremely frightened and kept locked up for some days before the indictment came out and Cawthorne was stark mad besides and ill in bed and the Justice Bradshaw came to Wyreside, instead of the offenders being taken before the Justices, the Justices of the Peace came to the offenders to take their bail.

A scandalous affair: – Richard Townley of Ortner, son of Thos and Elizabeth Townley, Fiddler and informer etc: It was by and through him that Cawthorne had such a scolding bout with my Father about my father chimeing in with folk at Ortner Smithy when they discoursed of Cawthorne's brave actions; and when Cawthorne had a great brustle[42] at Catshaw with Wm Brown and some others Richard Townley came down the fields with Ted Alstone and Townley and said he did not like such brustles and rough work and Edmund said 'No, they was very silly for doing so', 'if he was a gentleman he would get Samples to catch two or three hares privately and let nobody know, for John Samples was a very good hand and was here only a few days since catching two or three'. (all this he said in a joke) but Richard Townley went straight and told Cawthorne what Edmund had said and Cawthorne attacked Samples that very day and charged him with shaving[43] and such like. So this was Richard Townley's way of hastening such brustles and falling out. He, being one of Cawthorne's spies, attends Ortner Smithy very well to hear what people may say there, as well as in other places. He was talking with his best friend the Parson, James Bleasdale, curate at Wyresdale Chapel and schoolmaster at the Abbeystead and so James had expressed himself rather freely on some of Cawthorne's brave actions, such as Peter Tomlinson's & Thos Bradleys, and Richard went and told Cawthorne what the Parson had said. Cawthorne comes up in a day or two and gives James Bleasdale a good lecture and threatened to turn him out of the school. After that in a few days Cawthorne

42 i.e. confrontation, commotion.
43 i.e. defrauding.

went up again to the Abbeystead and catched [*sic*] James Bleasdale drunk at Henry Mason's where he had been all night. So then Cawthorne called on the other Trustees and appointed a day to meet at the School to turn James Bleasdale the Parson out of the School and they met accordingly. Thomas Townley being one he told Thomas Winder that he had scolded his son Richard for telling Cawthorne such stories, and so he went to the school with Cawthorne and they unanimously voted James out; Thomas Townley never standing up to the screen the injured Parson who was from his son Richard thus injured. I believe Richard has done more mischief and injured James Bleasdale more than he will ever do good in his lifetime. He never will do a good deed equal to counterpoise this ill deed. But he is spring of a bad stock and many of his relations have done things worse that what many men have been hanged for. (Straw, Sall, Mall, Wood, Sucks, Gloves, & narrow teeth). Cawthorne is also using his endeavours to have the Parson turned out of the Chapel but as yet he is unsuccessful. On the 8th of March the trustees to Cawthorne's will met at Lancaster to appoint a new schoolmaster in the room of James Bleasdale and there was only Rd Hathornthwaite, Thos Thompson and Anthony Blezard there and they did nothing. James Bleasdale the Schoolmaster having been sent for by Lord Archibald to come to Ashton Hall and he accordingly went thither and related his case to Archibald Hamilton and Major Clayton and they advised him to open the school again and begin to teach as usual and he should not be turned out, and told him not to be afraid for they would back him whatever it cost. They advised James Bleasdale to go to the other Trustees who did not sign his dismissal nor were acquainted with it and Major Clayton took James Bleasdale in his coach from Ashton Hall to Justice Butler's at Kirtland below Garstang, one of the Trustees, who gave James good encouragement. The day after James went to squire Wigelsworth, another Trustee, and was well received.

James Bleasdale accordingly as he had said opened the School on the 12th of March and begun to teach again. Cawthorne went sometime of the day and stormed at him but James said he would not be turned out, but the Trustees are to have a meeting at the School the 2nd day next week to appoint a new master. In the meantime disputes run high some being for James Bleasdale and some against him.

The Trustees met according to their proposal at the School on the 19th of March and James Bleasdale was teaching there and had got a lawyer from Lancaster to come and assist and he came and met the Trustees and they went to Hannah Drinkall's and consulted there James Bleasdale not budging from his place. The Trustees made nothing out but ordered James out of the school and he would not go. They then went and ordered Henry Watson off his farm, and then the lawyer Parkinson went to the school and all the neighbours being present by desire of James Bleasdale the Lawyer examined them respecting how their children had learned, and he took down in writing what they said. 6 or 7 of them, and then as many more agreed in the same day that their children had learned as well as they could expect and had liked the master well. And some of the neighbours testified that James had attended the School very well. The Trustees are to have another meeting on the 30th inst. Anthony Blezard was not at this meeting. Thos Townley signed a paper which James Bleasdale had testifying that his daughter had learned well and was well used. The next morning he went to get his name scratched out but James Bleasdale would not. He would consider of it a piece.

On the 23rd the trustees met at the Abbeystead and appointed a new Schoolmaster. He is called Hartley and comes out of Boland. The Trustees again ordered James Bleasdale out of the School, but he said he had possession and would consider of it a week or a fortnight. They then went and gave Henry Watson notice to prepare to quit his farm and when they had done Henry Watson's wife asked them if they had done but received no answer. She then said that they would not offer to quit until they had received notice 6 months before Candlemas. Thos Townley signed for the new Schoolmaster. This is his third vote. Some people call him signall, others say he has given a split vote.

Feb 28th: – All trade continues extremely bad and no employment for poor people, cotton and worsted spinning none is to be had unless the spinner be a very good one and those are paid at reduced prices.

At the beginning of February was married at Lancaster – Hathornthwaite from Boland to Dority Winder of Wyresdale. Hathornthwaite aged 81 years and Dority aged 80 years.

March: – John Pearey, schoolmaster, teaches in his house at Clevely. An old name on the left hand side of the road going to the Hollings standing two or three yards higher than the road. This man has an Ark which was infected with mites, so to get clear of them he got a quantity of dry Brackens and put them into the Ark and set them on fire and they blazed up to the top of the house and set the thatch and timber on fire. The man was so terrified that he had not presence of mind to shut the lid of the Ark. The neighbourhood was soon alarmed and all came, but too late, for the house was burned to the ground, but a good deal of Furniture was got out. The Ark however was cleared of the mites for it was entirely consumed. The house belonged to Lord Archibald Hamilton.

The Supplementary Militia are to meet at Lancaster on the 8th of this month and a part of them to be embodied. The Cavalry men are to be up sometime soon.

On 2nd of this month, Joshua Bebby, Assessor for Wyresdale brought about and delivered to all the Farmers and other in Wyresdale a paper to each of them on which their assessed taxes were set down which was, a pleasurehorse £3 12s additional, the old duty of 24/- being tripled and that added to the other makes the riding horse £4 16s a year. The workhorses are charged 12/- additional making on the whole 18/- per work horse. The appeal day is the 15th of this month at the Grapes Inn in Lancaster and I suppose a great number will appeal for they are charged far more than the Triple Assessed Tax Bill requires. For by the Act a man who pays between 20/- and 40/- assessed taxes was to be raised only one fourth of what he paid. The work horses not to be recorded in the Assessed Taxes and most in Wyresdale are in this class. How they came to make the Pleasure horse as it is called pay the Triple Assessment additional I cannot imagine. They might as well have charged it quadruple or quintuple as Tripple, but the Justices, the Commissioners, and the Clerks are a set of overbearing, tyrannic scoundrels and a curse in the country they live in. If the fools will not have much to pay, for there is a clause in the Act that if a man can prove that he is not worth £60 per year of a clear income he is to be exempt altogether except for work horses which are to be 18/- per year.

On the 8th of March the Supplementary Militia met at Lancaster and a number was lotted to be embodied forthwith. One half I believe was to be raised but some say 6 out of 10 are lotted to serve. For Wyresdale James Birkett was lotted for one, who serves for his father Richard Birkett. On the 10th of this month hundreds and thousands of the supplementary and others were at Lancaster. The supplementary are to learn their exercise at Lancaster. All accounts say the town is full of soldiers and Red Coats and some say that there is [*sic*] 4000 soldiers or of that profession in Lancaster and it at this time wears a very warlike appearance. The Lancashire Old Militia lying in Cornwall some of them are sent to drill these supplementary men at Lancaster. Some come from Bodmin to Lancaster in 5 days, a distance of 400 miles. One of these men told my father that he was at Bodmin and at the last first day at night knew nothing of coming here, set off the 2nd day morning and arrived at Lancaster the 6th day at night.

The wheaten penny loaf was on the 5th of this month 7oz 5drs and had been so since the 13th of January.

On the 5th of March was married Wm Procter son of Thomas Procter of the Higher Morehead, hatter, to Sarah Birkett, daughter of Wm Birkett of the Lower Morehead.

Some weeks since was married Richard Bibby son of James Bibby of Tarnbrook to – servant at Thos Bradley's. She has had a bastard child by William Willcock of the Lee.

Died the last week at Hathornthwaite a woman called Townley daughter of Thos Townley the night cap weaver.

The 15th of March was the appeal day at Lancaster about the Tripple Assessed Taxes and many out of Wyresdale appealed. Wm Holtkinson of Catshaw was charged about £7 additional and got about half of it taken off, he farming £150 per year. Joseph Whiteside got the additional duty taken off the Riding horse £3 12s. Thomas Procter could get nothing off, he being a farmer and master hatter employing 7 or 8 men constantly. All the lesser farmers got off who were charged with an additional 12/- per workhorse. Elizabeth Drinkall of Ortner appealed for the workhorses she farming £63 a year but she having some interest of money coming in she was obliged to pay 18/- per workhorse.

The 16th of March was the appeal day at Preston for the Amounderness Hundred and John Robinson of Dolphinholme was charged for 4 horses and farms £150 a year and he thought himself aggrieved though he had 5 horses of all and had not entered one a riding horse. In the whole he was charged 48/- additional so he went to Preston to appeal and the Commissioners found out that he was liable to pay for a saddle horse and charged him with one and surcharged him. The saddlehorse is now £4, 16s and the surcharge as much so instead of getting anything off he will have £9 12s more to pay. He is in a great rage and is for doing his neighbours that Kindness and force them all to pay if he can.

On the 17th of March was buried at Wyresdale Chapel William Pye aged 72 years.

There is about 800 militia at Lancaster and some soldiers besides. All the town full of them. At the Kings Arms 60 are billeted, at the New Inn 45, Bear and Staff 35, Boars Head 20, White Cross Tollbars 16 etc. It is supposed they will be marched from Lancaster in the course of the next week before the Assizes begin.

On the 24th of March the penny wheaten loaf at Lancaster weighed 6oz 13 drs.

During March there were very great disturbances in Ireland. That oppressed country appears to be on the eve of a terrible explosion. The consequences will be an emancipation from tyranny and oppression.

The French invasion much talked of and much feared by our Governors. If they do come they will probably swipe off all our droves.

April: – On the 10th was buried at Wyresdale Chapel Lawrence Pye of the Emmets in Wyresdale aged about 70 years.

Died a few days ago Parson Braithwaite of Ellel Chapel aged 80 years.

Died on the morning of the 10th at his house at Catshaw in Wyresdale, of the Gravel, Thomas Bamber, farmer, aged 70 years or upwards.

The worthy Trustees of the Abbeystead School met on the 21st of April at the Abbeystead for the purpose of turning the Master out and six of the Trustees appeared viz: – John F Cawthorne, Thos Thompson, Rd Hathorthwaite, Anthony Blezard, Justice Butler and Justice France. Three were for turning him out and the latter three for keeping him in, so nothing was done but another meeting was appointed for the next 5th day at the New Hollings. There was two Lawyers attended one on each side. It is said they mean to lay a new Indictment against the Schoolmaster for neglecting the School about a year since when there was a bit of a brustle with him but he promising to be more diligent he was continued on, but now they mean to try that point over again. Three of the trustees have set their hands to a paper agreeing to try this affair in the Court of Equity. They are Cawthorne, Thompson & Hathornthwaite.

It would almost keep a man doing to write down all Cawthorne's ill deeds, many times I resolve to write no more but as he is an extraordinary man I still follow him with my pen, but I sincerely hope the world will never be plagued with such another man and very much are they to be pitied who live under the paw of this tyrant. Because many of the inhabitants of the lower end of Wyresdale have spoken well of James Bleasdale and given evidence for him, Cawthorne to be revenged has decreed that the Turf got on the Abbeystead Fell shall be 5/- per fall, a very unreasonable price. For some years past it has been 2/- and before that for almost 100 years it was 1/6 per fall. Very few turf at this price will be got. The inhabitants may leave the place and flee from the tyrant of this land.

May 10th: – Today Thomas Goss an eminent Land Surveyor was buried at Wyresdale Chapel. A great number of persons attended. The Corpse was brought to the Chapel in a cart. He was the heaviest man I ever saw.

June: 23rd – At this time the Lancaster Canal is so low of water as to be impassable for laden vessels.

In the beginning of June Cawthorne begun to sink for a coal pit at Marshaw and was in great hope, but at the month end, being got 11 or 12 yards deep the water comes so fast into the pit that in a morning the pit is 8 or 9 yards deep of water which takes most part of the day to bail it out.

July: – On the 10th was buried at Wyresdale Chapel Richard Kelchin aged 77^1/$_2$ years. He had been ill 7 or 8 weeks and was waked with 5 weeks.

August: – On the 18th the Judges came into Lancaster. There is about 26 Crown Prisoners to take their trial besides many causes.

At Cawthorne's Coal Pit the Colliers have begun to bore and have got about 30 feet deep at this time.

Cawthorne is resolved to take in 200 acres on Marshaw Fell and has now one Thomas Buttle surveying and planning it out.

Most of the farmers at Marshaw have life leases of their farms and all together have a right to all the Fell, but gentle Cawthorne is resolved to take a great part of the best of the Fell from them without allowing them any recompense except curses and scolding and so much of the Fell being enclosed for his own use will be a very great detriment to the farmers.

The Canal Packet boat began to move on the 6th of this month. It sets off from Lancaster at 7 o'clock on the 2nd, 4th and 6th days in the morning and reaches Preston at 2 o'clock in the afternoon the same days and it comes back on the 3rd, 5th & 7th days, sets off from Preston at 7 o'clock in the morning and reaches Lancaster at 2 o'clock in the afternoon. Fares. For Cabin passengers 2/6 or 1d per mile. Steerage 1/6 or 1/2 per mile and for a short length 2d. Steerage 1/3 from Galgate to Preston. They have 4 changes of horses to convey the boat. The first stage from Lancaster for a man, a boy & 2 horses costs in wages 10/- for 4 hours work. The second stage, same strength 9/-. Third stage 8/6 & Fourth stage 10/-.

There is a fence between Cawthorne's Wyreside estate and Archibald Hamilton's land at Scott Farm. The fence is made by Cawthorne and some three to five feet in Archibald's land there was a row of trees which Cawthorne claimed and marked and would have sold them. Archibald also claimed them and felled them and lead them away. The question is as to whose trees they are. A special Jury came on the 21st to view the fence and the trees in dispute.

The trial came on on the 23rd at 9 o'clock and was decided in favour of Hamilton. There was a great number of evidences examined and some of those for Cawthorne swore bravely. Ingleby, an eminent Land Surveyor had viewed and planned the place for Cawthorne and was asked by the Judge if he had been sent to view the place without knowing anything of the dispute who he thought the trees would have belonged to, those who made the dike, or to the field behind the dike. He answered, the field behind the dike, that is Hamilton.

Counsel for the plaintiff Cawthorne was Cockel or Cockin. This lawsuit, it is said by Rob Mitchison, Hamilton's steward will cost Cawthorne £250. Hamilton paid his swearers 5/- per day and found them plenty of meat & drink.

Cawthorne's Coalpit: – Some men are boring and have got 30 yards deep but have found no coal as yet. Cawthorne was not tried at the Assizes for assaulting Peter Tomlinson but he traversed, and so it is put off till the next assizes.

On the 12th of August at 6 o'clock at night Richard Townley of Ortner came to our house and told us that on the 11th as he and his uncle were passing by

Galgate they were called to by Hannah Sanders, the Landlady, who told them that a gentleman in the House desired to speak with them that he had come down from London and was going to Wyresdale for there was a Prebendary of Chichester dead about two years ago whose name was John Heaps and that he was bred and brought up in Wyresdale until he was 9 years of age at which time he ran away and became a great scholar and Prebend of Chichester and that he died in the year 1796 aged 86 years and in his will he left £500 to purchase land and build a school and a home for the schoolmaster to live in and £50 per annum salary. On the 13th by 9 o'clock in the morning Betty Parkinson had found out that there was a woman in Wyresdale called Heap about the time that this man was born, about 1710, and that this woman was one housekeeper to one Master Bond of Durnshaw, schoolmaster at the Abbeystead, and that this woman had a child by Master Bond and that this child was the said John Heap very probably, and furthermore Betty Parkinson said that this housekeeper was her grandmother consequently John Smith is brother to this John Heap though it looks odd that a woman should call two of her sons John. Thos Winder was certain that he had heard tell of such a name in Wyresdale and he thought he was a hatter. My father was certain there was never a hatter of that name in Wyresdale. John Bateson aged 87 years and an inhabitant of Wyresdale most part of his time cannot remember any such name in Wyresdale in his time nor had as he knew heard tell of such a name.

The gentleman yesterday sent for James Bleasdale parson at Wyresdale and told him the story, and the Parson believed it was true. 3 o'clock: We have heard that the gentleman at Galgate has today sent for Parson Stuart of the Admark and he went & called at Cawthorne's as he was going Cawthorne said that the man at Galgate was an imposture and would have him turn back but he would not. Stuart went to Galgate and the man told him the same story and that there was to be 4 trustees appointed – one of whom was to be the Parson of the Place or of the Parish adjoining, and therefore appointed Cawthorne, James Bleasdale, John Tarnley[44] & Thomas Bateson, trustees. The master was to educate 20 tradesmens children. Today also this gentleman came to Wyreside to talk with Cawthorne about this Heap School but Cawthorne would not be seen of him. It is said that this man came in the Packet Boat to Galgate on the 11th of this month and that night he walked about to look at the country & went by Cawthorne's and to Galgate. Another time he had been at Wm Caton's shop and turned back the road was so rough he pretended that he could not get forward to Wyresdale.

23rd: – The man at Galgate that came about building Heap's School proved to be a Bailiff, one of John Fielding's men from London. He was several times about Wyreside but has not had the pleasure of seeing Cawthorne many of his journeys. Cawthorne is now forced to keep close quarters in his own house. It is said that there are ever so many Bailiffs about daily who wish to be doing with him.

September 5th: – About a fortnight since was married James Winder son of John Winder, blacksmith, to Mary Pye daughter of John Pye. There was about 20 persons at the wedding.

44 Townley.

Last week we received intelligence that 700 French were landed in Ireland and had taken the town of Killala and made some prisoners. Some reports made the French 1800. The official account says 700 and they were brought by 3 frigates, another account says 4 frigates. They brought a great number of arms and the country people were joining them. This week we have had an account that there had been a battle between the Invaders and General Lake, and the French beat their opponents and took 6 pieces of Cannon. The battle was fought at Castlebar, 25 miles from Killala. General Lake retreated 13 miles after the battle. His loss is stated to be very inconsiderable. Some accounts make the invaders to be 3000 or 4000 men mostly cavalry. The Bishop of Killala is taken prisoner.

Assessment: – There was a town's meeting held at Marshaw on the 10th for the purpose of taking into consideration the propriety of making the Poor Rate more equal than at present and it was agreed that the rate or sessment should be laid on more equal. The men appointed to this important business were Thomas Thompson of Lentworth, John Jackson of Greenbank and Joshua Bibby of Marshaw. Note: John Jackson and Joshua Bibby are Cawthorne's tenants so Cawthorne's land we may suppose will come off very lightly.

Died on the morning of the 11th James Shaw of Marshaw, farmer. He has left a wife & small children. He died of a surfeit from over much work & made his will only the night before he died.

22nd: – The French that invaded Ireland are taken prisoners, of all 842 men, by an army of 22,000 men who behaved with the greatest bravery, they being only 26 men to 1 man.

In this month there was a Supplementary Militia man lotted for Wyresdale in room of one man away and Robert Yates was lotted. He being in no Club[45] has got leave till this month end to find a man to serve for him and he got one which they refused, but gave him another week to find another.

October: – On the 5th Robt Gardner, son of James Gardner of Hearsonsike was leading turf of Hellfoot Moss to the Crag & as he was going along the road he met a lad with a wheelbarrow which frightened his horse so that it set off very fast & he ran & got hold of the Coker reins, the bits not being in the horse's mouth. The horse rushed forward and the cart run over Robert and broke his leg & made a large cut in the side of his leg. The horse ran forward for more than half a mile. Robert Mason saw the accident and went and carried Robert Gardner home upon his back.

24th: – Cawthorne's Coal pit: They have got through rock and into a softer sort of shilla and are now about 80 yards deep. They propose to go 100 yards deep.

The Cotton and woollen trades are said to be much better this month than for some time past.

Cawthorne is for having 300 statute acres enclosed on Marshaw Fell and has let part of the wall building from the present copy nook to the Trough foot to John Gornal limeburner at The Sikes who is to get the stones, lead them, & make the wall for 8/- per Perch of 7 yds.

---

45 Local militia ballot clubs provided insurance for substitutes for members who were called up to serve in the Militia.

An Estate beside Scotforth Moor belonging to Rawlinson sold this month for £2835 to Hume – 58 acres of land statute measure and is now in the possession of John Spaulton as tenant thereof.

November 5th: – A ship that sailed from Lancaster last week met with a storm on the coast of Ireland & it thundered and lightened. A flash of fire struck many of the sailors blind for a considerable time but they recovered again. The foremast and bowsprit were broken down and fell overboard yet all the men escaped unhurt.

Lancaster Castle which has cost £20,000 repairing and beautifying is now reckoned to be the completest and finest piece of architecture in Europe. So said a gentleman who has made the grand tour of Europe twice over.

New Assessment: – The persons appointed to make a new valuation of Wyresdale and make a sessment more equal than the present one is have performed their job and great alteration is made in the sessment. All the farms at the lower end of Wyresdale have less to pay in the new sessment than in the old one. The new Sessment is £36 which is $2^1/_2$ d in the pound on the value put on the rent of the land by these men. At Catshaw their sessment is nearly double. At the Abbeystead nearly the same as before.

At Cawthorn's Coalpit they have got into another solid rock, by boring at the depth of about 67 or 68 yards and pretend to be in great expectation of a good bed of coals.

Sometime last week a bailiff from Preston came to Wyreside and wanted to see Cawthorne for a certain gentleman at Preston well acquainted with Cawthorne he pretended wanted a gamekeeper and with this pretence he came to Wyreside with two dogs and told his errand & was immediately let into the Hall to Cawthorne & there he told Cawthorne a fine story about wanting a gamekeeper but Cawthorne begun to suspect something & begun to be very stormy & made towards the room door, but the bailiff got us [*sic*] & set his back to the door, pulled out a pistol and swear he would shoot.

The cotton and worsted trades are said to be better this month. Worsted spinning is 11d per lb for 24 hanks and 12d for 26 hanks. At Dolphinholme factory the latter end of this month they begun to spin day and night.

It is said that a bed of coals a yard thick has been found in Bowland near Newton at Larnhill.

Cawthorne's borers are in a solid rock.

Cawthorne's enclosure on Marshaw lot proceeds. All the wall is let to persons to build at 7/6, 8/- and 9/- per rood. The wall to be a yard thick in the bottom and 7ft high.

December: – The week ending the 15th was a most stormy week. A very violent East wind blew for 6 days and did an amount of damage chiefly in thatch and it is the whole subject of conversation at this time.

On the 28th Benjamin Clough a servant at Cawthorne's old and infirm went with a cart to Emmets for a beast that had died & as he came back up the brow below the Smithy at Ortner he was riding on the cart head & not taking proper care he let the horse come too near the browside & the cart threw over and he flew down the scar and was found motionless lying in the bottom and was carried to Robert Clarkson's with very little signs of life but in an hour he came to himself and was no great deal worse for his fall having no bones broken nor much bruised. The Horse and cart were found part of the way down the Scar held there by an Oak of 10 or 12 years growth, and could by no means be parted in that situation for no one durst venture near except on the upper side. The horse's legs were trapped fast in the backband & could not be loosed. So having fixed divers ropes to the cart & wheels & horse they were all let down the scar together but for all the ropes they went with a terrible rush & the cart was broken to bits. The horse received no harm. But the little Oak which providentially stopped the Cart & horse Old Ben had been killed on the spot. The place where he went down is almost perpendicular & 8 or 9 yds down.

1799

January: – On the 14th was married at Lancaster Church James Bleasdale, offici- ating Minister at Wyresdale Chapel & Schoolmaster at the Abystead School in Wyresdale to Betty Tomlinson of Lentworth, the daughter of John Tomlinson farmer, late of Pilling, James Bleasdale aged 38, Betty Tomlinson aged 20.

On the 16th died George Ward, butcher at the Abbeystead after an illness of about 8 days, aged about 67 years. His arm swelled amazingly and looked like as if it had been boiled for many hours & it was the cause of his death. He was very little respected or beloved. By his death Cawthorne comes in possession of a little farm which George held in life lease at Marshaw.

Early in the morning of the 19th the Barn of John Bibby, Weaver, of Borwicks in Wyresdale was burned down together with 4 spring calving cows, a large quan- tity of hay, 2 carts, the turf house and all the Turf. The loss to John Bibby is esti- mated at £50 or upwards and will reduce him to beggary. The loss to Landlord Thomas Townley is estimated at £50 or £60. The rent of the farm is only £22 a year.

On the 27th was buried at Wyresdale Chapel Ellen Yates of Scorton in Lower Wyresdale, a relation of Townley's of Ortner and maintained by the town of Plumpton, aged about 70 years. A good natured woman and a notable talker to herself.

Some time ago, since the great wind the 16th of last December the Landlord of the Public House at the Oakenclough, called Wearing, was thatching, & he shift- ing the ladder for a new gang & it holding at something he gave a stronger lift & the ladder broke and he fell backwards and fractured his skull. He died in about 4 days after and only fell about 5 or 6 feet. He had been Landlord only part of a year.

February: – 23rd Died lately William Riding of Marshaw, a young man, some- times deranged in his understanding. He died suddenly at Whalley after drinking oft a dobbin of rum.

March: – On the 20th was buried at Wyresdale Chapel a child of John Pye's of Oozlethorn.

On the 26th the Assizes began at Lancaster. There was 26 Crown prisoners in the list to take their trials. They were all tried before the 30th. 4 were condemned to be hanged, 10 acquitted, 1 Remanded, 1 fined 1/- & imprisoned for 14 days, 2 fined 1/- & imprisoned for a year. 1 imprisoned for 6 months 1 imprisoned for 2 years. Admitted Kings evidence 1. No prosecution 2. No Bill 1. Transported for 14 years 1. Transported for 7 years 1. Of all 26 prisoners, besides Cawthorne & Law.[46] Stone.

April 1st: – JF Cawthorne and Tom Stone were tried today at Lancaster assizes for assaulting Peter Tomlinson and taking a gun from him and found guilty were fined 6s 8d. The first week of April was very winterly. Frost, cold, & snow have seldom exceeded what has been this week & driving snow so late in the spring can not be remembered.

Funeral: – On the 5th an old woman at Hearsomsike the weather proved so stormy that only 2 or 3 persons attended & so the funeral was postponed till the 6th, when it being market day at Lancaster & some who should have been at the funeral going to the Market they blocked up with snow that a great strength was required at 2 o'clock the funeral set off from Hearsomsike to Cockerham. There was about 30 men and 6 or 7 women present. We went over the fields over hedge and dyke to the 5 Lane ends and the road from the Crag being so full of snow that we durst not venture on it it being level with the fences all the way.

James Simpson of the Fell End in Lower Wyresdale should have been buried on the 6th at Sledburn but the road is so blocked up with snow that it was put off to the 7th.

In the trough of Bowland 30 men were employed in cutting a road through the snow on the 6th and on the 5th at night 40 men were employed in cutting a road from Galgate to Lancaster and they got it finished that night.

This storm of snow has drifted an abundance of sheep and it being just the time of lambing it has done very badly as may Ewes have lambed under the drifts and some lambs have got out of the snow and their Dams have been found dead under the snow & many lambs lost.

On the 27th there was 3 men hanged at Lancaster.

At the end of the month the scarcity of Fodder continues increasing and is nearly all expended and grass there is none. The ground is as bare as possible and cattle are greatly famished. Hay is sold at 1/- per stone and very little can be got at that price. There is accounts that many cattle have been hungered to death. It is said that meal and wheat will be dear this summer for the scarcity of fodder has caused the farmers to give their cattle corn in such quantities that it is reported that the cattle eat more than the people. Potatoes have advanced in price this month 2/ or 3/ per load great quantities having been frosted and more given to the cattle. This scarcity of fodder extended all through May & had been very scarce from the beginning of the year. This is the most backward spring ever remembered.

46 Thomas?

At the end of May the Cotton Trade was very brisk and several people were learning to weave at the Sheel in Lower Wyresdale. Worsted spinning by the hand is very low, only 10^1/$_2$ per lb of 24 hanks.

June: – On the 8th was buried at Wyresdale Chapel Thos Bibby of Marshaw. On the 1st he was well and getting turf on the Fell. By his death a farm at Marshaw goes out of Lease in possession of Joshua Bibby. On the same day there died at the Bond Yate Thomas Gornall.

On the 1st was buried at Wyresdale Chapel. Old Mitchell of the Oakenclough aged 99 years, maintained some time by the Parish.

Last week was married at Lancaster Andrew Richmond (miller) aged 75 to Peggy Lawrence aged 35. (Andrew died in October 1804).

In the beginning of June was buried at Wyresdale Chapel the wife of John Fanshaw of Ellel and when the Corpse was brought to Ortner John Fanshaw said 'Let us take her through the fold,' & so they carried the corpse through John Townley's fold by the house door. It being considerably further that way than on the road made folks wonder why the funeral went that way, & for what reason or purpose it was done is not yet resolved.

August: – During the week ending the 17th was buried at Wyresdale Chapel Jane Morley of Hathornthwaite. She died of a fever which prevails at this time.

During the week ending the 24th there died at Wyreside old Ben Clough for 24 years servant to JF Cawthorne.

On the 17th there was the greatest flood in the Ribble remembered for many years. It overflowed much land, laid corn flat & washed a deal of hay away.

In the week ending the 24th an estate in Ellel called the Lower Cragg belonging to Cawthorne was sold to Ed Rigby for £881, let for about £35 a year and the stone quarry made as much for some years.

September: – In the first week an estate called Ward Field was sold to John Townley of Ortner with a house, barn & gardens, in all 17 acres of land for £1950. An Estate situate at Boursaugh belonging to Thos Jefson sold to Hinde for £1970. 22 acres of land, 2 houses & a barn.

October: – The night of the 6th excessively heavy rain and a very great flood. In Wyre it was the greatest that has been for some time & much land was overflowed, potatoes spoiled, dykes & walls washed down. Cawmill weir is almost totally washed away & it is said that it will cost £40 to repair it. Cleveley Mill wear was washed out and Cleveley Bridge washed down – a wood footbridge – There has only been 3 greater floods in the Wyre in the last 12 years viz 17th of August 1787; the 28th of October 1787; and on the 22nd of August 1793. In the Ribble it was an exceedingly great flood & vast quantities of corn swept away.

The cotton Trade is rather lower this month. It has been very brisk all this summer and a deal of folk have learned to be muslin weavers in Lower Wyresdale at the Sheel in particular and more are entering on this winter. This trade had like to have overspread Wyresdale once before, just at the breaking out of the war. The merchant trade is very bad at this time, all the West India produce being fallen in price.

December: – A town's meeting was held at Marshaw. All the pensioners wanting more salary and it was agreed to give them 40 per head more than they had before considering the times are very hard and dear.

1800

January: – On the 1st at night George Johnson of Lancaster liquor merchant was travelling about Black Burton on horseback. The storm was very furious and the snow became very deep in some places so that he was forced to dismount and was something unwell and much benumbed with cold and he lost his horse and went on foot till he came to a farm house where he called them up & told them who he was and that he was almost starved to death so they let him into the house where he told them many particulars of his journey and being then very cold he desired they would give him a glass of Rum which they did. They then wished him to go to bed to where one of them had just got out so he went and soon fell asleep and waked no more. He died.

On the 11th inst was buried at Wyresdale Chapel Ellen Procter daughter of Thomas and Agnes Procter of the Morehead in Wyresdale, aged 22 years. She died of a decline having been ill for a very long time.

On the 25th inst there was a Riot at Lancaster as follows: – The Price of meal was uncommonly high and considerably on the advance and when all was sold but a load or two that a man had asked more for it than a market price which enraged the poussards (poor women of the town) so much that they said that he deserved to have it taken from him and he gave them very saucy language and said he hoped meal would be £5 per load in a very little time which made the women very angry and they seized his load of meal and threw it down rent or tore the sack and begun to divide or sell the meal, which I cannot say, some say they sold it at 6lbs for 1/- . A Party of Dragoons was in the town and was immediately drawn up under arms and a party I suppose of Lancaster Volunteers entered the Town Hall with their bayonets fixed and drove all the women out of the Town Hall and as I understand before much of the meal was carried away. The Cavalry then paraded the streets for some hours to keep peace and quietness among the women.

Further particulars of the Riot – It is said the man that was mobbed asked something more than market price and the buyers bid considerably less and so he said he would not sell it but set it up for he should not wonder if it was £5 per load before the month end and the mob was so enraged that the man got away as fast as he could. In an hour or two it was thought provident to take the meal, 3 loads, from the Town Hall to the Bear and Staff in the Penny St and so it was put in a cart and they got Ralph Parker to drive the cart and a party of soldiers went with it. At Penny St about the Bear and Staff a vast crowd of people was collected together and the Dragoons rode through them many times which caused great thrulching and brustling among them and many were forced against the sides by the press of the crowd and the windows on both sides of the street were broken by people being forced against them. The owner of the meal was guarded out of the town by the soldiers and then the mob followed after and pelted him with mud and stones.

Jan 31st: At Dolphinholme Factory about 3 weeks ago the gudgeon of the Waterwheel broke & they were 3 or 4 days in getting a new one made & fixed. The weight of the new one was 540 lbs.

There was never perhaps so much cause to fear a famine or at least a great dearth of Corn as at the present period, from the backwardness of last spring and the unparalleled coldness and wetness of the last summer which caused an universal failure in the crops of corn of all sorts so that meal at this time has advanced to £3 10s per load. The farmers have thrashed upon the whole more than usual of their crops at this time of the year and sold all the meal that has been made. In Scotland and Ireland there has been but indifferent crops and in America the crop is light owing to the hotness of the summer there. In Canada it is said to be a good crop. The Merchant trade is very bad indeed, they can sell nothing except to loss and the markets are greatly overstocked in the West Indies with British goods. The Cotton Trade is also bad at this time both for the Manufacturers and the labourers. Many weavers are turned off. The Hatter's trade is very bad and shoemakers have also experienced a great stagnation in their trade.

February 8th: – Died about the middle of this week John Parker of Hathornthwaite aged 93 years. He had been married 61 years and has left a widow nearly as old as himself. He was maintained by the Parish for a great number of years last past.

February 22nd: – The Publicans at Lancaster in consequence of the high price of malt and hops thought it proper to raise the price of ale from $1^1/_2$d to 2d per dobbin and from 3d to 4d per pint which displeased their customers so much that they would not drink at all. Three or four men would go into a Public House and call for every one a Dobbin of Ale and when it came would enquire how much the price must be and being answered 2d they told them to take it back and immediately walked out of the house. At one much frequented house during 3 days they did not sell half a dozen dobbins of ale so when the people would not drink as usual the Publicans were obliged to drop to the old price again after holding it at 2d per dobbin for 3 days and selling scarce any at all. However I suppose they can scarce afford it at the old price malt being 48/- per load 24/- per windle and hops £15 to £16 per cwt.

It has been in contemplation for some time by some of the inhabitants of Wyersdale to enter into a subscription and raise a sum of money to buy meal flour and potatoes and to sell the same again to the poor and labouring people within Wyresdale at reduced prices.

In Ellel that plan has been carried forward and about £40 subscribed and they have bought meal at market prices and sold it again to the poor at 6lbs per 1/- that is at the rate of 40/- per load. Potatoes they have sold at 1/- per score. Their regulations are to sell to all who are needful residing within the Township of Ellel whether they belong to them or not. That each person entitled to this charity shall have 3lbs of meal per week so that a man and his wife & 6 children receive 24 lbs of meal per week for which they pay 4/- only which according to this days price would only purchase 11 lbs of meal.

Subscribers to Wyresdale List [*includes*] JF Cawthorne 0,5,[s],5[d], R Hawthornthwaite 0,5,5, Betty Hawthornthwaite 0,1,1, Peggy Hawthornthwaite 0,1,1, Thomas Thompson 0,4,4, John Townley 0,5,5, Thomas Bateson 0,2,2, Timothy Cragg 0,1,1, Thomas Cragg 0,2,6, Timothy Cragg 0,2,6, Richard Cragg 0,2,6, David Cragg 0,5,6, Parson White of Lancaster £2,2,0, Parson Thomas of Lancaster £1,1,0...[total of 49 names]. Note: The total amount of the subscription was about £48.

Peter Bramwel and Joshua Bibby having received upwards of £40 by subscription to buy meal and potatoes to sell to the poor in Wyresdale at reduced prices having bought a quantity of meal and potatoes 6d per 20 lbs and disposed of about a load and a half of meal and above a load of potatoes. They are very careful in the distribution of this meal and potatoes though as well as any other township it is sold to old folk and children only and those who are maintained by the town. Everyone entitled to this charity is to have only 3 lbs of meal per head for 6d or 6 lb of potatoes in lieu thereof at 6d per score. About 66 persons received of this allowance today. This allowance is for 1 week and is agreed that it shall be distributed once a fortnight, on the 4th day of the week in the afternoon at the Abbeystead.

Thomas Mason of Forton sold part of his land a few months ago by auction. He has now sold the remainder to wit 2 acres of land and a very good modern built house for £200 and a suit of clothes to Thos Huntington.

March 12th: – A Fast and Prayer day today by order of Government to pray to God that he – would be mercifully pleased to help them to kill most part of the French this year and also help them to restore the Bourbon family to the throne of France again. It was not much observed in this country.

Edmund Winder has bought an Estate of Land in the Field called – [*sic*] Hall for £1600 it being about 36 acres of land and a well built place.

The Assizes begun at Lancaster the 25th inst and the Calendar of the Crown prisoners amounts to 69 prisoners a greater number than ever known.

At the end of March most kinds of trade were very bad excepting the calico weaving which is very brisk again.

At Dolphinholme Factory the wages allowed to the labourers employed in the factory is too small to afford them a maintainance and sometime a family are out of provisions of any sort for several days and children crying about the Factory for want of Meal and falling down of fair hunger. Some people had given several shillings worth of bread amongst them in the factory, Hadwen the master would not allow them any more wages nor give them bread. They might live without bread, he did, and so might they, he said.

Richard Kerr of the Factory shopkeeper buys very bad meal, half of it barley, at 74/- or 75/- per load and sells it at only 2³/₄ lbs for 1 lb which amounts to 87/- per load so he gets a very great profit out of these poor people and he being in league with Hadwell[47] gets his Bills paid off at the Counting House every pay day

47 Hadwen.

so that many a poor family receive not a halfpenny, for their Bills equal what they are allowed as wages.

April 5th: – The Assizes at Lancaster ended this week, the list of provisions 72, of which 12 were sentenced to death, 14 transported for 7 years, 11 no Bill, 13 acquitted, 10 fined and imprisoned 3 turned Kings evidence & 3 to remain in Custody. The rest fined & discharged and some imprisoned in the House of Correction. It is thought that 10 or 11 will be hanged. There were 46 causes to be tried at this Assizes.

April 12th: – As the dearth of provisions is very great at this time perhaps it will not be amiss to say something about it every week and this week at Dolphinholme Factory it has been agreed that the people employed therein shall be served with meal by Rd Kerr at 4lbs per 1/- and the Company to make up the loss and that they shall have rice at 3d per lb of which much is used at this time in making rice porridge. There are many poor families that buy barley flour and bean flour to make bread and upon the whole there is now in this country many a hungry mortal.

On the 19th inst six men were hanged at Lancaster for forgery and robbing the post boy.

On the 24th was buried at Wyresdale Ellen Cragg daughter of William Cragg of the Abbeystead aged 11 or 12 years.

April 26th: – At Lancaster an advertisement was posted up on the Town Hall that a great number of the inhabitants had entered into an agreement not to give more than 1/- for a lump of Butter nor suffer their servants and recommended the same to all the inhabitants which hurt the market considerably so that scarce any was sold at 12 o'clock, part being sold at 16d, 15d, 14d, and much at 13d¹/₂ but in the afternoon about 2 o'clock it rose again to 14d & 15d, so although a great stagnation was made in the market there was none sold at the price fixed. After the market was over there was scores of people wanted to buy and could get none and many a bit of grumbling there was and scolding and the sellers took it upon them to be very saucy and very scornfull and ridiculed the buyers very much and vexed a great many of them so that after the market was over I heard several of the Townspeople say that they had been sauced and abused worse than a shame to see it.

May: – On the 15th was married at Lancaster Thomas Cragg to Betty Kelsall daughter of Wm Kelsall of Durnshaw in Wyresdale. There was 16 invited guests at the marriage and the marriage certificate was signed by 36 witnesses. We dined at the Bear & Staff and paid 18d each for dinner. At night the new married couple went to a cottage house at Greenbank to reside there some time.

Caw Mill Wear is to be made up again this summer, wood being now felling for that purpose. Joseph Whiteside joining with Tomlinson at the Mill etc for the time to come.

June: – On the 8th died John Butler, shoemaker, of Galgate of a fever. He will be a very ill missed man.

On the 9th died Joseph Whiteside of Forton late of the Humble Bee host in Quernmore, being ill only 5 or 6 days.

There are at this time many folks ill of a violent fever at Galgate and several have died of it. This fever having been about near half a year in this country.

June 27th: – Report says that 7 ships are arrived at Lancaster laden with corn, 5 of which are from Liverpool and 2 Dutch Daggers.

July: – The fever at Galgate still continues with much violence and many are scarce expected to recover and it is feared that the whole of the inhabitants will have it before it is settled. There has died at Galgate, John Butler, John Welch's daughter, a servant maid Molly Bell & her husband & Robert Butler's wife at the Milkehurst a woman has died of the same fever there are 20 now ill of it at Galgate.

August 5th: – John Wilson, Carpenter in Cockerham son of Wm Wilson died last week aged about 26 or 27 years & has left a widow & 2 children.

August 20th: – was married today Timothy Cragg to Jennet Parkinson, daughter of Richard Parkinson of the Hazleheads.

An estate of land situate at Clifton Hill in Forton belonging to Wm Corless of the New Hollings was sold by Auction the latter end of this month to John Drinkall of the Castle of Trim in Wyresdale for £1650 it being 26 acres of land.

September: – On the 7th was buried at Wyresdale Meeting Agnes Procter wife of Wm Procter, hatter, of the Moorhead aged 58 years, of a decline.

October: – On the 10th most of the Cogs in the Cogwheel broke. From the 10 to the 29th two and sometimes three millwrights were employed in repairing the wheel and other machinery in the Mill at 5/- per day and a quart of ale each. On the 29th they started the mill again and it is reported to do very well.

December 12th : – Richard went this morning with Robert Mason to Lancaster with 2 carts met some carriers from Kirkby Lonsdale by appointment at the pinfold Barham Lane near Lancaster at 6 this morning with 15 load of meal which Robert Mason had bought at Kirkby yesterday and which was carted in the night for fear of mobs at Lancaster and elsewhere. Being a Badger now is somewhat a dangerous trade.

1801

January: – On the night between the 9th and 10th of this month a barn at the Yatehouse in Ellel was burnt down and 24 head of cattle consumed therein. It is supposed to have been wilfully set on fire by some person or persons yet unknown. A large quantity of hay and corn was reduced to ashes. The damage to William Gardner the tenant is estimated at £350. The Yatehouse Barn was still on fire on the 11th. It is supposed that there was 3000 persons to view the ruins this day.

[*No entries between February 1801 and May 1809*]

1809

May: – On the 1st Ellen Gibson widow of Richard Gibson of Quernmore dropped down dead on the home floor.

On the 5th was buried at Wyresdale Chapel Richard Pye of the Ouslethorn[48] in Over Wyresdale aged 76 years.

On the 3rd a young man in Cockerham called Dawson hanged himself.

On the 10th the yearly town's meeting for the township of Over Wyresdale was held at Marshaw and the Overseer and Constable Benjamin Raby brought in their accounts. In the last year they have collected in assessments about £620 and of it £99 18s was paid in Constable Rolls. The Church Rate was also paid out the Poor Rates which was about 320. We found a deal of fault with their accounts and the expenditure of the money. John Pye of the Fellside engages to do the office of Overseer and Constable for this year for £21.

June: – On the 18th of this mth Samuel Fielden of Lancaster was drowned in attempting to cross the sands from Ulverston to Lancaster.

September 30th: – About a month ago the large Ash tree was felled at Lentworth in Over Wyresdale. The Bole and measurable limbs amounted to 224 feet: a piece of the Bull end 12 feet long was 80 feet and sold to a Blockmaker in Lancaster at 4/3 per foot, came to £17. William Wilkinson took it to Lancaster on the 15th of this month. It was by a great deal the largest tree in these parts.

October: – About the beginning of this month William Carter of Eccleston died. Formerly he was a farmer in Hashaw but had for some years been maintained by the Township of Wyresdale.

On the 16th died at William Caton's in Ellel old Dority Caton widow of Thomas Caton of Hashaw in Wyresdale. For some years maintained by the Township of Wyresdale.

Also on the 16th died Francis Parkinson of Brow Top in Quernmore. A poor miserable rich man. Reckoned to be worth £16,000.

1810

February: – On the 2nd was buried at Wyresdale Meeting Ann Birkett wife of William Birkett of the Higher Morehead in Wyresdale.

On the 27th was buried at Wyresdale Meeting Ann Jackson of Quernmore Brow Top who died suddenly aged 82 years.

April 7th: – Last week died Isaac Jackson, commonly called Little Isaac of Marshaw, but lately Whalley aged about 86 years. By his death the farms of Bartholomew Pye and John Harrison go out of lease which have been held by his life a long time.

---

48 Ouzel Thorn.

About the middle of this month died Ellen Freenlah of Quernmore aged 98 years. The oldest person in these parts.

About the same time Thomas – commonly called Old Thomas Shirriton of Quernmore aged 88 years.

On the 23rd died John Harrison of Lancaster aged 35 years. For several years noted as the most drunken man and saddest vagabond in all Lancaster.

May: – On the 7th the yearly Town's meeting for the Township of Over Wyresdale was held at Marshaw and was well attended. The accounts brought in by John Pye overseer of the Poor and Constable for the last year were satisfactory. The money expended last year was about £582 of which £107 was for constable rolls. £19 for church rate. He had collected 8 assessments at £68,18,8 each.

At this meeting John Bleasdale was let to Robert Fort at 3/4¹/₂ Robert Scales to Thomas Walmsley to have 44/- a year for wages besides finding him clothes. Kitty Townley was taken by Edmund Hall for 2 years, he being to find her clothes for that time for nothing. Bec Austin's daughter taken by Rd Holden for 2 years to find her in clothes and the town to give him 39/- per year. John Swindlehurst taken by Richard Topham for 2 years at £5 per year. The town to find clothes.

On the 10th was married at Lancaster Joseph Pye son of James Pye of Speight Clough in Wyresdale Weaver to Agnes Pye to the top of the Emmets in Wyresdale weaver. At this marriage was 26 persons present 20 of whom were of the name of Pye.

On the 2nd was married James Pye son of James Pye of Speightclough in Wyresdale shoemaker to a servant woman at Thos Walmsley's, Lentworth, in Wyresdale. A woman it seems of spirit.

On the 12th of this month Wm Carr of the Throstle Nest in Nether Wyresdale had his house burned down. Set on fire by sparks blown up the chimney & setting the thatch on fire.

This week died John Salisbury of Nether Wyresdale Cotton Weaver, of a fever.

Also Ann Bamber of Great Eccleston, widow of John Bamber, formerly of Catshaw in Over Wyresdale.

July: – On the 12th I got up stones in the nook of the mean old causeway made in former ages. It was about 4 feet wide, the stones 2 or 3 feet square & some of them 2 feet thick. The biggest I met with was 4 feet long 3 feet wide and 2 feet thick = 24 foot of stone. It must have been a vast [*sic*] of work to get such stones to the place and as it were to flag with them.

1816

February: – On the 6th died at the York Retreat, Betty wife of Thomas Cragg of Damas Gill Side in Wyresdale.

INDEX TO *WALTER SHAIRP'S MEMOIR*

Walter Shairp and the Liverpool Blues have been excluded, for references to them appear on most pages.

INDEX TO *THE WRITINGS OF THE CRAGG FAMILY OF WYRESDALE*

PLACES

SUBJECTS